What people are saying

This is what the gals of our generation are craving—a big sister, rooted in God's Word to guide and encourage them as they're going. Heather has listened to the heart of her readers and partnered with the Lord to give them varied voices and biblical wisdom to spur them on. Not only would I suggest reading this book, I'd massively encourage every woman I know to buy a handful of copies for the girls in her life!

—Jess Connolly
author of *Wild and Free* and *Dance Stand Run*

Surviving my teenage years without this book or a big sister is only God's grace in my life. *Letters from a Big Sister* is full of raw and honest stories from women who have learned lessons the hard way, and have seen and tasted the goodness of God through it all. Heather's wisdom to exposit each story and attach actionable responses is a gift that will persevere the hearts of today's teenagers.

—Jamie Ivey
best-selling author of *If You Only Knew*
and podcast host of *The Happy Hour with Jamie Ivey*

This is such a brilliant and beautiful resource for teen girls! I love the compassion, kindness, and wisdom that fill these pages, and the engaging nature of the book. I wish I'd had this to encourage me through my development in my younger years. We need all the help we can get. Heather, thanks for offering the next generation the opportunity to stand on your shoulders and access the heart and wisdom of these incredible ladies.

—Candace Johnson
Senior Leader, Bethel Church

I love everything about this book! Every girl needs the wisdom and safety that can come from heartfelt and honest conversations with a big sister—one who has already navigated through the many challenges of life, made hard decisions, known heartbreak, and learned from the mistakes she has made in her own life.

Life isn't just a journey from here to there, but from who we are to who we are becoming. This book is full of wisdom and insights about how to journey well and become the magnificent woman God has created you to be.

—Helen Burns
tor, Relate Church

LETTERS FROM A

Big Sister

Shared Wisdom to Encourage and Equip Teen Girls

heather boersma

LETTERS FROM A BIG SISTER
Copyright © 2019 by Heather Boersma

Scripture quotations marked (NIV) are taken from the Holy Bible, New International Version®, NIV®. Copyright © 1973, 1978, 1984, 2011 by Biblica, Inc.™ Used by permission of Zondervan. All rights reserved worldwide. www.zondervan.com The "NIV" and "New International Version" are trademarks registered in the United States Patent and Trademark Office by Biblica, Inc.™ Scripture quotations marked MSG are taken from THE MESSAGE, copyright © 1993, 1994, 1995, 1996, 2000, 2001, 2002 by Eugene H. Peterson. Used by permission of NavPress. All rights reserved. Represented by Tyndale House Publishers, Inc.

Printed in Canada

ISBN: 978-1-4866-1767-8

Word Alive Press
119 De Baets Street, Winnipeg, MB R2J 3R9
www.wordalivepress.ca

Cataloguing in Publication may be obtained through Library and Archives Canada

For my grandma, Mary Wiebe.
Thank you for showing me what it looks and feels like to be a loved daughter of God.
Your schatze, Heather.

Contents

Acknowledgments

First of all I'd like to thank my amazing husband, Alex, for convincing me that this book really was a good idea! If it wasn't for your constant encouragement and creative strategies, this book never would have happened. Thank you for always cheering me on, but also for loving and believing in all of our sisters as much as I do.

To every single woman who contributed to this book—Jess Connolly, Jessica Honneger, Jamie Ivey, Jenna Kutcher, Kristene DiMarco, Tiffany Thurston, Leslie Crandall, Rach Kincaid, Carrie Lloyd, Lauren Vallotton, Alisha McKay, Shezza Ansloos, Hannah Giddens, and Summer Wright—thank you. Some of you I know well, and others I've never met, but taking the time to share your heart and experiences gave me the fuel I needed to keep going. Thank you for believing in me, this idea, and most importantly, our little sisters.

A special thanks to my best friend Alisha McKay for being my person, my safe place, my bestie. I love you so much, and look—we're doing it! We're writing our first book together after sixteen years of talking, dreaming, and praying about it. Here's to many more to come!

The visual aspect of this book was so important, but I'm no designer! Thank you, Grace Alexandra Taylor, for taking my ideas and turning them into reality. Your style guide brought my vision to life and helped create this amazing finished product. I really couldn't have done it without you.

To every photographer who contributed images, thank you—especially my cousin Matt Wiebe and friend Rosie Haberl. Thank you for sharing your gift with this audience. Your beautiful images bring the words on the page to life.

A big thanks to the whole team at Word Alive Press, in particular to my project manager and friend, Sylvia St.Cyr. Thank you for believing in me and this book. Working with you has been such a joy.

To all of the women who have been big sisters to me—including my mom, Aunt Sandy, Grandma Wiebe and Grandma Derksen, Amanda Cook, Stephanie Dyck, Hannah Giddens, Lori Burke, Sherry Ansloos, Adrienne Pearson, Kate Feucht, and Leslie Crandall—thank you for the courageous lives you live. Each one of you is a letter I love reading and learning from every single day.

My Jesus. Thank You for loving me perfectly, believing in me entirely, and never ever giving up on me. Your words are life, whispering breath into my lungs to keep me going every single day. This book is my worship to You. I hope it's a sweet sound in Your ears.

Sister! I am so glad you are holding this book and reading these words! I've been thinking and praying about this moment for months and now it's really happening. You're here. I am so happy you're here. I genuinely wish I was sitting there with you having a heart to heart over some ice cream (my fave!), but this is a close second.

The reason I'm so excited this book is in your hands is because it is *full* of stories and wisdom from some incredible big sisters who love you as much as I do. When I asked these women to share their stories and wisdom with you, they all said an enthusiastic, "Yes!" Each one *wanted* to be a part of this book, not to tell you how to live your life, but to remind you that you're not alone.

Being a teen girl isn't easy. There are so many emotions, pressures, and relational dynamics that are really complicated. And sometimes it can feel like there is no one to talk to about these challenges. That's why we've written this book. We want to walk with you through the hard things and hopefully give you some tools to get to the other side without too much pain or heartache.

I believe in you, sister. I believe that God loves you more than you know and has a plan for your life that is beyond anything you could imagine. You bring something special to the world that no one else can bring and I want you to show up and release that light as fully as you possibly can.

But I know there are things that hold you back. Fear, hurt, shame, negative self-talk—I struggle with all of these things too. But I've had big sisters help me overcome, and I want to do the same for you. So let's do this!

What to Expect

Each chapter of this book starts with a letter from a different big sister on a specific topic. In her letter, she shares a story of a challenge she faced as a teen girl and what she wishes she would have known then that could have helped her through that time.

Following each letter, I share some biblical and practical wisdom on the same topic, as well as some steps you can take to apply what you're learning.

Each chapter ends with a section called Soul Selfie. We live in a time when everyone's an expert at taking the perfect selfie. You can barely go anywhere without seeing someone whip out their phone, hold it up above their head at just the right angle, and snap a few pics. We know how to tilt our chins in order to capture the perfect image of our face, but do we really *know* ourselves at all? This section of the book is all about taking a moment to get a snapshot of more than just our outward appearance. We want to get to know ourselves on the inside too. Don't rush past this—it might just be the most important part of the book.

I really do wish I could be there with you, but fortunately we can still connect on social media. You can find me on Instagram (@heatherboersma) and connect with other sisters reading this book (@lettersfromabigsister). Please come, introduce yourself, and let me know what you think, or if you have any questions. You can also email me at heather@heatherboersma.com. I look forward to hearing from you.

Love your big sis,

Heather

YOU ARE

never alone

_____

chapter one

Dear sister,

I'll never forget this one bonfire.

I was in high school almost a full year after I'd met Jesus. There was no gentle on-ramp for me and Jesus; I was head over heels with Him from day one. I'd spent so much time running from Him and hiding from Him that once He beckoned me out into the light, I couldn't stay away. I'd wake up each morning with a slow smile spreading across my face as I remembered: *Hope.* I had hope now. *Grace.* I was forgiven! *Peace.* It wasn't my job to worry any longer! *Identity.* I did have a place in the world.

I loved Jesus and I was also learning to love all the things that came with Jesus.

Like community, for example. I'd made a few sweet Christian friends who were fun and life-giving. I was learning to love the Bible, finding for the first time that a slow, sweet joy would spread through me every time I put my hands on the soft leather cover. And I was learning *all* about Christian boys. They were so much nicer than the other guys I'd dated! They took me on real-life dates rather than sneaking me somewhere dark. They wanted to talk to my mom and play with my baby sister and help with our family yard sale. Plus they were still just as cute as the non-Christian boys, so all in all following Jesus was going pretty awesome.

Except one night I was at this bonfire and my new Jesus-loving boyfriend wasn't with me. It was a group event, but he had to work. I was so bummed. And my closest friends? They couldn't be there either. Old non-Jesus-loving Jess would have just not shown up, but it seemed weak to back out just because none of my best people would be there, so I still went.

I stood around the bonfire, watching the flickering bits of orange float into the sky, and stuffed my nose deep into my jacket to inhale that beautiful campfire smell. In that moment, I decided that was my favorite smell on earth. The weather was just perfect that night, brisk and chilly—but not uncomfortably so—and as I took it all in, I felt a strange, deep sadness well up in me. I really, really, really wished my friends and my guy were there to experience it with me.

I could have made new close friends that night, bonded with other girls. To be honest, pre-Jesus-Jess might have even made a new boyfriend that night, just to avoid having to experience it alone. But the new Friend and Comforter who lived in me was stirring and moving, calling me to a new pattern, a new way of thinking. I moved away from the group, folded my knees into my chest, and looked up at the sky while the Holy Spirit did His work in my heart. This is what He was telling me: "Jess, you're actually *never* alone."

Wherever you go as a Christian, whatever you experience, whether it's tragic or magical, you take a Best Friend with you. You have Someone to talk to. You have Someone to listen to everything you're feeling, thinking, dreaming, and pondering. You have Someone who understands.

You're actually never alone.

It's been more than fifteen years since that picturesque bonfire. I married that Jesus-loving young man and we've had four kids. A few of those newfound Christian friends stood beside me on our wedding day. Some I still get to catch up with, others I haven't seen since.

Friends have come and gone as we've moved and changed communities, but I've never been alone. In the scariest and darkest moments—in hospital waiting rooms or in meetings where my stomach violently churned with anxiety—I haven't been alone. On dark nights when my seemingly closest companion has felt distant or has been in his own heavy season, I haven't been alone. When friends have hurt me, betrayed me, and kept their distance because I've hurt them, I haven't been alone. When I got an exciting email and no one was around, when I saw a beautiful view, when I experienced the glory and grace of new life and new seasons, I haven't been alone.

And sister, if I could tell you one thing, if I could grab your face and encourage you with one simple truth, it would be this: you are never alone. You always have access to Someone who's a trustworthy friend and good listener. Not only that, but you have access to the God of the universe. The Father who formed the world and made up the very idea of you has made a way for you to boldly enter the throne room of grace with confidence. Day after day. Hard moment after hard moment. Celebration after celebration. Your Father is there, waiting to experience everything with you and He will be your absolute greatest companion.

Friends are going to come and go—boys are certainly going to come and go—but Jesus isn't going any-where. And in His presence, there is fullness of joy. In His arms, there is comfort beyond any human comparison. In His Word, there is wisdom that would put all the best friend advice you could ever receive to shame. In His worship, there is freedom. In His family, there is belonging. In His grace, there is dancing. In His holiness, there is belonging. In His mission, there is privilege.

And you get to go. You get to be with Him. You get to be His. You are never alone.

Love your sister,

Jess Connolly

Thoughts from Heather

I love Jess's story because it reminds us that we can actually be comfortable and satisfied with just Jesus. That doesn't mean we ignore the people around us or isolate ourselves from community, but the truth is that nothing and no one will satisfy our souls like friendship with Jesus. Embracing this truth brings so much freedom into our lives. When we find ourselves in situations like Jess did at the bonfire, instead of feeling awkward because we don't know anyone, we can just relax and be present. We don't need to perform for love, because the truth is that we are already so loved!

One of my favorite verses is Psalm 73:25–26, which says, *"Whom have I in heaven but you? And earth has nothing I desire besides you. My flesh and my heart may fail, but God is the strength of my heart and my portion forever"* (NIV). This verse reminds us that everything we need is found in relationship with our Creator. We might feel temporary satisfaction when people like us, but that feeling never lasts. As quickly as it comes, it goes and leaves us wanting more.

But when God tells you of all the things He loves about you—that satisfaction doesn't fade.

We aren't the only ones who struggle with wanting the acceptance of people around us instead of being satisfied with friendship with Jesus. The disciples had a similar conversation to the one we're having here today. It says in Luke 9 that the disciples, the ones who knew Jesus the most and experienced His loving presence on a daily basis, got into an argument over which of them was the greatest. Can you believe these knuckleheads? Here they were, hanging out with the Way, the Truth, and the Life—God in human form—and they were still busy chasing after position, promotion, and approval.

But Jesus didn't judge or condemn them. Instead He said, *"Whoever welcomes this little child in my name welcomes me; and whoever welcomes me welcomes the one who sent me. For it is the one who is the least among you all who is the greatest"* (Luke 9:48, NIV). I don't think Jesus was trying to tear them down to size. I think He was just reminding them of who they really were. They weren't nobodies who needed to elbow their way into the spotlight to get a little love; they were His beloved children. Jesus was reminding the disciples then, and us now, that even when we feel like we're at our worst, we are still great to Him. Even when we mess it up, He still loves us and calls us His own. It's not our greatness that draws Him, but rather our need.

So what does it look like to make Jesus our everything? How do we keep our hearts from looking to the people around us for love and comfort rather than having our needs met in friendship with God? How do we, like Jess, become comfortable in our own skin whether or not we're surrounded by our friends and family and their acceptance?

Here are a few of the things that have helped me find my satisfaction in God, and reminded me that I'm never alone.

Go to Him first. It's tempting when we face a challenging situation or great celebration to go to our friends first and God second. But what would happen if instead of running to our best friend or boyfriend to process life's circumstances, we actually ran into the arms of Jesus? He wants to be that friend for you. He wants to be the one you unload on. He wants first dibs on your heart.

When you go to Him first, you get your needs met in a way that allows you to have a more healthy connection with the people around you. Instead of needing your friends to fill that void, you'll find what they give you is a blessing, a bonus. But if you expect your friends to meet your needs on their own, they'll always come up short. It'll be frustrating for both you and them.

Jesus is waiting for you to come to Him. Whether it's been a long time or just a little while, take some time today to bring Him your joy and your mess, your thankfulness and your disappointment.

Are you tired? Worn out? Burned out on religion? Come to me. Get away with me and you'll recover your life. I'll show you how to take a real rest. Walk with me and work with me—watch how I do it. Learn the unforced rhythms of grace. I won't lay anything heavy or ill-fitting on you. Keep company with me and you'll learn to live freely and lightly.

—Matthew 11:28–30, MSG

Ask good questions. God wants to speak to us, but we often have only one-sided conversations with Him. I don't know about you, but I grew up thinking that prayer was me calling God and leaving a message on His voicemail. I never expected that He might actually have something to say in response.

When we take time to ask good questions and actually listen to His answer, we'll grow a real friendship with Him. Here are two of my favorite questions to ask God: "What are you doing in this situation?" and "How can

I partner with what you're doing?" Asking these questions helps us find His perspective on our situation so we can partner with Him.

> *Don't bargain with God. Be direct. Ask for what you need. This isn't a cat-and-mouse, hide-and-seek game we're in. If your child asks for bread, do you trick him with sawdust? If he asks for fish, do you scare him with a live snake on his plate? As bad as you are, you wouldn't think of such a thing. You're at least decent to your own children. So don't you think the God who conceived you in love will be even better?*
> —Matthew 7:7–11, MSG

Practice being present. Next time you find yourself in an uncomfortable situation where you don't know anyone, or if you feel awkward and out of place, practice being present by doing the following. Instead of thinking about yourself and how out of place you might feel, imagine that Jesus is beside you. Picture Him with you and feel the comfort of His love and acceptance.

As you become aware of God's presence and love, look at the situation through His eyes. What's going on in the room? How are other people feeling? What can you contribute to people around you who might be feeling alone? This will help you not feel so awkward, anxious, and insecure, and it will also allow you to be more fully yourself. Who doesn't want that?

> *God is our refuge and strength, an ever-present help in trouble.*
>
> —Psalm 46:1, NIV

As you read over these tips, which one stands out the most? Ask God which one is the most important for you right now and be intentional about applying it in your life this week.

You are so loved, little sis. And you are never alone.

Love always,

Heather

My Prayer for You

God, I thank You for Your love and desire to know Your daughter intimately and be known by her. I pray that she would find her satisfaction in being close to You, that she would physically feel Your presence and love surrounding her, even when she feels alone. Help her to remember that she is never alone now that she has You. Remind her of the things You've spoken to her through Jess's story and the rest of this chapter. Amen.

Soul Selfie

ways to connect with God

Here are some ways to put what you're learning into action this week. You can do one per day, do them all at once, or whatever works for you!

Day 1: Bullet Journaling

Use the prompt "Ways to Connect with God" and jot down your ideas in point form. No need for full sentences or perfect handwriting. Pull out some colored pens or pencils and get messy!

Day 2: Live the Letter

Pencil It In (little step)

Take time this week to go on a mini-date with Jesus. It could be a fifteen-minute walk or even a solo stop at a coffee shop. Pay attention to how you feel on the date. Is it hard, awkward, or uncomfortable? What did you like about it and what did you dislike? Why?

Put It In Ink (bigger step)

Take a whole morning or afternoon to hang out with Jesus. Turn off your phone and just bring your Bible, journal, and pen. Go somewhere quiet and see what happens. Resist the urge to plan it all out or fill every moment. Take time to just sit, listen, and observe. Spend some time journaling about the experience later. What did you love? What did you find difficult? What did you learn?

Day 3: Reflection

1. I feel most alone when _____ because _____

_____ .

2. One way I can connect with God the next time I feel alone is

_____

_____ .

3. What's one area you would like to grow in making Jesus your everything? (For example, go to Him first, ask good questions, weigh words, and be present.)

_____

_____

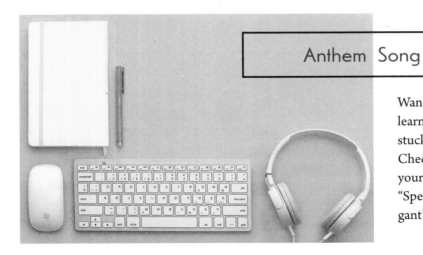

Anthem Song

Want to remember the truth you've learned today? A great way to get truth stuck in your head is through music. Check out these great songs to remind yourself that you are truly never alone: "Speak to Me" by Kari Jobe and "Extravagant" by Bethel Music.

Day 4: Letters from a Big God

Don't just take our word for it—your Creator has a lot to say on this subject. Here are a few verses you can check out to learn more about God's perspective. As you read, ask the Holy Spirit to point out an important verse for you and write it down in your journal, on your mirror, or on a post-it note you can put someplace where you'll see it every day.

Deuteronomy 31:6—8, Hebrews 13:5

Day 5: Note to Self

Write a short note to yourself or God about the things you've learned from this chapter. What points really stood out to you? What do you want to remember as you go into this next week? How has this chapter changed your perspective about God or yourself?

Dear _____

be real

_____

chapter two ↑

Dear Sister,

One of my best memories of being a teenager was having sleepovers with my best friend. Almost every weekend we were swapping houses, staying up way too late, creating fun dance routines and being silly. My parents even put a spare mattress under my raised twin bed so that my best friend would always have a spot when she spent the night. We were totally devoted to each other, and at the time I thought this was normal. Little did I know that the Lord was giving me a taste of what it felt like to be *seen*, *heard*, and *known*.

After we graduated high school, my friend and I stayed connected, visiting one another at college and writing old-fashioned letters back and forth. At Bible college, I met a lot of people from totally different upbringings and experiences than mine. It blew me away how many of them were in pain from hard relationships and didn't know how to share their heart with God or others. I seriously considered going into a career in Christian counselling because I constantly found myself listening to people's problems and helping them to hear the voice of God for themselves.

During this time, I remember calling my parents to thank them for the love and support they'd raised me with, that I had taken for granted.

I missed my old friends desperately but slowly began to find some amazing women who shared my core values for authenticity and encouragement. It was a beautiful season of discovering more about who I was and who Jesus was to me. I even met the man of my dreams, which is a whole other story. We got married after graduating and started into full-time ministry. Life seemed perfect!

But when my husband and I started our ministry, I could feel myself gradually changing to meet the expectations of the people around me. It wasn't a conscious decision, but I stopped fully being myself. The friendships from my teenage years, and those from college, far exceeded the friendships I now surrounded myself with. I just couldn't seem to connect with people.

Since I believed that leaders couldn't show their struggles to the people around them, I only had my husband to confide in. But I longed for the sort of friendships I'd experienced earlier in my life. I knew it was possible. I clung to the Lord like never before and I can honestly say that my friendship with Jesus grew so strong in those years of struggle, of not feeling seen or known by the people around me.

I felt like my strong personality and firm beliefs weren't welcome and I began to shut down the fun and free-spirited side of myself. The authentic me was being pushed out and replaced by a milder, toned-down version of me. My heart was crying out for deep and meaningful connection, but I was wearing a plastic mask in order to fit the mold of what I thought others expected me to be.

It's painful to hide your true self, isn't it? And plastic is a dangerous thing to hide behind because it suffocates anything it covers. When I showed people this plastic-mask version of myself, their interactions with me just bounced off. I wasn't able to absorb anything, good or bad.

But the power of vulnerability is that when you take off the mask and allow people to see the real you, they can connect to who you really are. Only when you take that mask off can you have real connection with the people around you.

God has some thoughts about the power of being real too. When God created Adam and placed him in a garden, He intentionally left Adam totally naked. No clothes, no accessories, just his birthday suit. Can you imagine? We don't know how long Adam walked around naked, but it was long enough for him to name all the animals. That would definitely take some time! The point is that Adam was naked and alone with God for a while.

This shows us how important it is for us to get to know God in a very vulnerable way. It isn't a quick or shallow process, but rather a lifelong journey of allowing yourself to be seen by God. Yes, He already knows everything about you, but how much more connected do you feel to Him when you share with Him your deepest, darkest secrets? There's a reason we were first created naked—God doesn't want anything hidden between you and Him.

Vulnerability isn't just about sharing the messy, crazy side of yourself that you're reluctant to let people see. There's something deep and powerful in sharing the gifts, talents, and dreams of your heart. And it's just as important to reveal your strengths as it is to reveal your weaknesses. Fully expressing the truest form of yourself is the most vulnerable act of bravery you could ever choose.

My dear sister, live out of the naked, unashamed version of who you are. Enjoy the journey of discovering more of who He is and you will find who *you* truly are too. Allow the friendships in your life to be guided by authentic living and true encouragement. Our culture could really use more real women to demonstrate what it looks like to truly champion each other. We might even be able to change the world together!

Much love and grace,

Leslie Crandall

Thoughts from Heather

If we want to walk in the kind of vulnerability Leslie described in her letter, we need to understand the difference between being transparent and being vulnerable. In our world of Instagram and Facebook, just about everyone is good at being transparent. We share so many details of our daily lives that people feel like they know us even if they've never met us. They know the outfit we're wearing, what we ate for lunch, and even what mood we're in. Often we share these intimate details with strangers before we even tell our families and friends.

But being transparent isn't the same as being vulnerable.

One definition says that being transparent means "having thoughts or feelings that are easily perceived."[1] When we're transparent, we allow people to see what we're thinking and feeling. But we don't necessarily invite those people to speak into our situations or *affect* the way we think and feel. We're honest but not necessarily open to being influenced. Transparent people say, "You can see me, but you can't affect me." Because of this, transparency doesn't necessarily build real connection.

According to another definition, the word vulnerable means "susceptible to physical or emotional attack or harm."[2] When we're vulnerable, we not only show people what we're thinking and feeling, we actually give them some degree of power to impact those thoughts and feelings. Vulnerable people say, "You can see me *and* you can affect me." This allows us to grow real and deep connections with others.

I'm not suggesting that you make yourself vulnerable to just anyone. In fact, I don't even think you need to be transparent with everyone! But I do think there's power in learning to be vulnerable with a few safe people. We all need to have friends who really know us, and who we allow to speak into the sensitive areas of our lives.

---

1   "Transparent," *Oxford Living Dictionaries*. Date of access: November 8, 2018 (https://en.oxforddictionaries.com/definition/transparent).

2   "Vulnerable," *Oxford Living Dictionaries*. Date of access: October 24, 2018 (https://en.oxforddictionaries.com/definition/us/vulnerable).

Vulnerability is powerful, little sis! I know you're afraid that showing your true self will make people judge and reject you, but the opposite is true. Being vulnerable with the right people can bring you healing, connection, and freedom.

Share Your Strength

Being vulnerable isn't just about bringing those dark secrets we carry into the light. It's also about sharing our dreams and showing our strengths. I love this quote by author Marianne Williamson:

> Our deepest fear is not that we are inadequate. Our deepest fear is that we are powerful beyond measure. It is our light, not our darkness that most frightens us. We ask ourselves, Who am I to be brilliant, gorgeous, talented, fabulous? Actually, who are you not to be? You are a child of God. Your playing small does not serve the world.[3]

One thing that feels more frightening than confessing my struggles is sharing my big dreams. Recently I was a student in ministry school and every week we met in groups of about sixty-five people to learn, share, and grow together.

On one particular Wednesday morning, our pastor wanted us to go after fear by being vulnerable with one another. One of the activities we were asked to do was to write down one of our big dreams on a whiteboard for everyone in the room to see. Even though I'd known these people for a couple of months already, and most of them had seen me cry, this felt incredibly vulnerable for me.

What if they think my dreams are crazy? I asked myself. *What if they think I can't do it? What if they smirk when they read my dreams because they seem so unrealistic?*

But the assignment was to kick fear in the face, so I marched straight up to that whiteboard and wrote, "My dream is to travel all over the world preaching about Jesus in stadiums. I'm going to pray for people and see them be healed of cancer."

Even as I finished the final words, I felt my face flush with embarrassment. How could I really think I would ever see these things happen? The biggest group I'd ever spoken to was maybe five hundred people and the only thing I'd seen someone be healed of was a headache.

---

3   Marianne Williamson, "A Return to Love: Reflections on the Principle of A Course in Miracles," *Marianne.com*. Date of access: November 8, 2018 (https://marianne.com/a-return-to-love/).

Instead of laughing, though, my friends read my words and nodded their heads in agreement. Some of them smiled at me as if to say, "I can see it. You'll totally do this one day." Others came up to encourage and pray over me for the ability to pursue these things until I saw them become reality.

To my surprise, not one person scoffed. In fact, I felt as though they believed in me more than I believed in myself. This gave me strength and courage. Had I not been vulnerable enough to share these dreams with my community, I would've missed out on that encouragement and those prayers. When we hide our light from the world, we aren't doing anyone any favors, especially not ourselves.

What About Humility?

I can almost hear some of you asking this question as you read about my whiteboard moment. What about humility? If we start to own our strengths and share our dreams, won't we become prideful?

Can I be honest with you, sister? As girls, I don't think we have a problem with too much pride. If anything, I think our problem is with false humility. Author Rick Warren says, "True humility isn't thinking less of yourself, it's thinking of yourself less."[4] For too long we've believed the lie that humility means brushing off compliments or giving out the spiritual-sounding answer of "It's not me, it's Christ."

But the truth is that God isn't honored more when we stay small and silent. God gets the most glory when His daughters are living in the fullness of who they were created to be. So let's stop worrying so much about pride and start owning the greatness He's placed inside of us. And if God needs to humble you, and your heart is open to Him, trust me, He will.

---

4   Rick Warren, "Quotable Quote," *Goodreads*. Date of access: November 8, 2018 (https://www.goodreads.com/quotes/201236-true-humility-is-not-thinking-less-of-yourself-it-is).

Can You Take a Compliment?

As we move toward becoming more vulnerable with our weaknesses and strengths and begin to build deep connections with the people in our lives, it will be so important to learn how to receive compliments. When we're given compliments, we often want to brush them off by saying things like "Oh, that was nothing" or "It's not me, it's just Christ in me." I'm not saying that God isn't the one who put those beautiful gifts in you, but when you brush off the life-giving words people speak to you, you take the power out of their words and miss the gift that person is trying to give you.

True friends aren't going to compliment you just to flatter you or puff you up, but to encourage and strengthen you. In order to receive that encouragement and strength, you need to accept their words and allow them to take root in your heart. One of the ways you can practically do this is by saying a genuine "Thank you!" without making any excuses. If you want to take it a step further, you can say, "I agree with that."

What we give our agreement to, we give our power to. So when you agree with words of truth, you give power to the truth in your life.

If this feels uncomfortable, think about how often you agree with words that aren't true about yourself. We often have conversations in our heads about all the ways we're failing and don't measure up. Why are we so much more comfortable telling ourselves negative stories instead of rehearsing the truth?

So next time you're given a compliment, try saying to yourself, "Yes, I agree with that" and just see what happens.

Love always,

Heather

My Prayer for You

God, thank You that when You made Your daughter, You made no mistake! You created her with all of her strengths and all of her weaknesses, and You love her totally and completely. Please give her the courage to be vulnerable with the people in her life. Help her to know that taking off her plastic mask and showing people her heart is safe because You are always with her. Help her to be vulnerable, not just transparent. Bring people into her life who will see her through Your eyes and call out the gold in her and help her to grow into the amazing woman You've created her to be. Amen.

Soul Selfie

people tell me I'm good at...

Day 1: Bullet Journaling

Use the prompt "People Tell Me I'm Good At..." and jot down your ideas in point form. No need for full sentences or perfect handwriting. Pull out some colored pens or pencils and get messy.

Day 2: Live the Letter

Pencil It In (small step)

Share the list you made from the bullet journaling part of this chapter with one or two of your closest friends or family. Try not to be embarrassed or leave things out. Remember that sharing your strengths is a powerful way to practice being vulnerable with others.

Put It In Ink (bigger step)

Email three to five of your closest friends or family and ask them what they think you're good at. Then, if you're feeling really brave, ask them one area where they think you could grow. When you read their responses, pay attention to how their feedback makes you feel and journal about it. Was it harder to hear the strengths or the weaknesses? Why do you think that is?

Day 3: Reflection (fill in the blank)

1. Some of the friends I've allowed to see the "real me" are: _____

_____

2. The hardest thing about being real and vulnerable with people is: _____

_____

_____

3. One way I want to grow in this area is: (sharing weaknesses, sharing strengths, receiving compliments, etc.). Why? _____

_____

_____

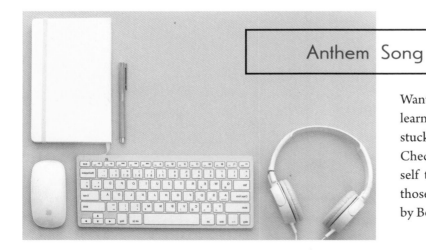

Anthem Song

Want to remember the truth you've learned today? A great way to get truth stuck in your head is through music. Check out this great song to remind yourself that you can be real with God and those around you: "You Make Me Brave" by Bethel Music.

Day 4: Letters from a Big God

Don't just take our word for it—your Creator has a lot to say on this subject. Here are a few verses you can check out to learn more about God's perspective. As you read, ask the Holy Spirit to point out an important verse for you and write it down in your journal, on your mirror, or on a post-it note you can put someplace where you'll see it every day.

Psalm 139:1—4

Day 5: Note to Self

Write a short note to yourself or God about the things you've learned from this chapter. What points really stood out to you? What do you want to remember as you go into this next week? How has this chapter changed your perspective about God or yourself?

Dear _____

YOU DON'T NEED A

best friend

chapter three

Dear Sister,

Right now I have the kind of best friend who makes you wanna say #goals. We don't live in the same city, but we're super close. She checks in with frequent FaceTime calls, and we text each other emoji updates throughout the day. We take trips together with our husbands, and our kids get along like long-lost cousins. We take turns holding each other's arms up when we grow tired and weary. We don't call fighting "fighting"; we call it conflict and we handle it. We've learned how to celebrate each other's accomplishments without jealousy or resentment. We honor each other and spur one another on. We run on mission together, side by side, advancing God's Kingdom and listening for what He's asked us to do—even if our callings look different from one another's.

It sounds amazing, right? But if you feel jealous, please stop right there. The reality is, she and I have known each other for more than a decade and only became close over the last few years. Our friendship has grown very slowly and intentionally.

And there's something I need to tell you that I'm afraid you won't like, but I've got to say it anyway: you don't need a best friend right now.

When I look back on my high school years, I can see that I couldn't have handled what I have now. I wasn't ready for a friendship like that. I might have ruined it, actually. I tried to attach myself to one friend after another, hoping to find a special kinship that would get me through those tough years.

Instead I wound up getting hurt and hurting others. I cared so much what people thought of me that I often paid little attention to the people themselves. I knew Jesus and I had a general idea of how to love people, but I had an even stronger need to belong and be liked. I'd flip through my Bible at night and show up to youth group sporadically, hopeful for a sense of peace about my place on earth, but my relationship with God was just another slice of my very full, very compartmentalized life. Instead of asking Him to meet me and teach me more about Himself and love people out of that place, I'd lie in bed and strategize ways to do better with friends the next day at school. I'd ask Him to help me be more accepted.

I took my cues on everything from college to boys from friends I only knew on a superficial level. I made decisions affecting my future based on what I hoped would get me the most approval from people. I made it through those years relatively unscathed, thank God, but not without some regret and a little baggage. It's strange to think about how isolated and lonely I felt. People were generally kind to me, but most of the time I felt unsure, insecure, and a bit rushed.

The thing I've learned about high school is that it's normal to feel a little unsure and insecure. But it shouldn't feel rushed. There are no shortcuts to a life that feels full and worthwhile. There are no easy formulas to feeling secure in your skin and valued by the people around you.

If you're willing to put in a little effort and time, though, there's one way to get there. It's a slow, steady formula. It's called "abiding."

First, you must grow to understand that there's a God who made you fearfully and wonderfully, a God who designed you for relationship with Him.

Second, you must somehow get your brain and heart and soul around Jesus's instructions from Matthew 6, which tell us to seek first the Kingdom. Why? Because the same God who made us also happens to love us and already knows what we need. When we keep our eyes on Him, He promises to give us all the other things we worry about—like friendships and confidence and wisdom. In the meantime, though, all we have to do is seek the Kingdom.

When our focus is on God and His feelings toward us, we stop caring so much about what people think. We stop longing for that one best friend, because we know that our identities are secure as daughters of the King. We make decisions based on where we feel Him leading us, not based on where the crowd is going. We dig into the Word and we show up to live in authentic community not because we ought to or because we hope it'll fill some hollow space in our gut, but because those are the places where we see Jesus more clearly.

Slowly, surely, day after day, we find ourselves more sure of our step and direction. We begin to walk more confidently in our calling as disciples and disciple-makers, and we reach out with more maturity to the gals around us.

And just like that, at just the right time, God may bring us a best friend. You know, the kind of best friend you realize you didn't need before but you sure are glad to have now. The kind of best friend who makes a life of seeking first the Kingdom that much sweeter.

Love your big sis,

Rach Kincaid

Thoughts from Heather

One of the things I love most about Rach's letter is how honest she is about the challenge of building solid friendships as a teenager. I desperately wanted a best friend when I was a teen, but I never really had one. It was discouraging not to have a person I could go to for anything and everything, someone I could laugh myself silly with or cry with until my face was red and blotchy. You may already have that person—and if you do, that's amazing. You're truly blessed. But if you're like Rach and me and you don't have it yet, don't be discouraged. Please don't give up. Don't buy into the lie that if it hasn't happened yet, it never will.

The truth is, all the best things in life are worth waiting for—and often we do have to wait. But just because it hasn't happened yet doesn't mean it won't. It also doesn't mean something is wrong with you. Just as it takes time to find the right spouse, finding a friend you'll want to run with for the rest of your life isn't meant to be a quick and easy process. The truth is that the people you partner with will shape your future in ways you can't fully understand right now. It's important to be a little picky!

I didn't meet my best friend until I was eighteen and out of high school. But now we've been best friends for over fifteen years and it's easy for me to say that it was worth the wait. But I know it's much easier for me to say that on this side of the experience. I have my best friend now, so how can I really relate to where you're at? The truth is, I can't—other than from memory.

But I can give you some advice on what you can do while you wait.

Rach briefly mentioned two ways to get your heart ready for finding an amazing best friend and also becoming the kind of best friend you're wishing for. A big part of finding a great person to run with is cultivating your own heart and life into something that draws people to you in return. Let's have a closer look at her advice.

Understand Your Value

The first tip Rach mentioned in her letter was growing to understand that there's a God who made you fearfully and wonderfully, a God who designed you for relationship with Him.

If we don't value ourselves, we really don't have anything to give someone else. If we go into friendship looking for that person to give us value, the relationship will fall short. We'll always feel disappointed, and our friend will feel the pressure of that impossible task. This is a surefire way to kill a budding friendship.

But if we can grasp the truth that we have value simply because God created us, regardless of whether we're hearing it from others, we will bring an incredible gift into all our friendships. When we truly receive the revelation of His love, we will begin to give that love away. A person who knows their own value is irresistible.

It's not enough to just believe it in our heads, though. We need to know it in our hearts as well. Psalm 139:13–14 says, *"For you created my inmost being; you knit me together in my mother's womb. I praise you because I am fearfully and wonderfully made; your works are wonderful, I know that full well"* (NIV).

You may have heard this verse before, but have you ever noticed the last five words? The author, David, not only acknowledges that God did a really good job when He made him, he also says it's a truth he knows full well. This shows us that it's not enough to believe God thinks we're worthy of love—we actually need to *agree* with Him.

There is so much power in our agreement with God's truth. David could have said, "Your works are wonderful, but you seemed to have made an exception when it came to me." It sounds a little silly, I know, but don't we say things like that all the time? We believe God is the Creator and that He made everything beautiful, yet we seem to think we're the exception to the rule. This kind of thinking is exactly what keeps us from embracing our value. It keeps us from being able to develop deep and healthy connections in our friendships.

Seek Him First

Rach's second piece of advice is to get your brain and heart and soul around Jesus's instructions from Matthew 6, which tell us to seek first the Kingdom. Let's have a look at Matthew 6 and dig a little deeper into this idea and figure out why it's so important when it comes to building deep, lasting friendships.

Therefore I tell you, do not worry about your life, what you will eat or drink; or about your body, what you will wear. Is not life more than food, and the body more than clothes?...
But seek first his kingdom and his righteousness, and all these things will be given to you as well.
—Matthew 6:25, 33, NIV

In this passage, Jesus teaches a life-changing truth: when we spend our time chasing after all the things we need and want, we end up running in circles. Sometimes we get what we want and hustle hard enough to make it happen, but more often than not the things we're trying to get are out of our control. Instead of finding that perfect best friend, we end up pushing people away with our desperation and insecurity.

But when we first chase after God and the things that are important to Him (His Kingdom), we can't lose. Not only does He promise to take care of all the things we need and want, but we'll also grow closer to Him and become more fully ourselves. It's a win-win scenario. You can't lose when you put your pursuit of God before any other pursuit in your life. It's not about Jesus and a best friend, Jesus and our dreams, Jesus and the perfect husband; it's just about Jesus. Everything else is meant to be icing on the cake.

So instead of trying to find that person you can share your life with, the best friend who can be with you through it all, aim your efforts at making Jesus that person. The truth is, you will never find a better friend than Him. Even when you meet your person, she'll let you down. She might move away. She'll grow and sometimes even change. But Jesus will never let you down, never leave you, and never change.

Love always,

Heather

My Prayer for You

God, thank You that You are the best friend we could ever have and Your friendship is available to my sister, right here, right now. Please surround her with Your love today. Help her to know that she doesn't have to be loved and accepted by her peers to be loved and accepted by You. Remind her of all the things You love about her. Give her the wisdom and courage to become the kind of friend of You've created her to be. Amen.

Soul Selfie

best friend qualities

Day 1: Bullet Journaling

Use the prompt "Best Friend Qualities" and jot down your ideas in point form. No need for full sentences or perfect handwriting. Pull out some colored pens or pencils and get messy!

Day 2: Letters from a Big God

Pencil It In (small step)

Reach out to a friend you aren't super close with and do something to grow your friendship. It could be an encouraging text or note, a kind comment on Instagram, or even an invitation to hang out. The point isn't to turn that person into your best friend, but to practice reaching out for connection.

Put It In Ink (bigger step):

Send an email to your three closest friends and ask them these two questions: "What is my strength as a friend?" and "What's one area where I can grow as a friend?" I know these are scary questions, because no one likes to hear constructive criticism, but if you're serious about being good best friend material, this exercise will help you grow into that.

Day 3: Reflection

1. What's one quality you possess that makes you a really good friend?

_____

_____

2. What's one area where you want to grow to become an even better friend?

_____

_____

3. What's one thing you can do this month to start to grow in that area?

_____

_____

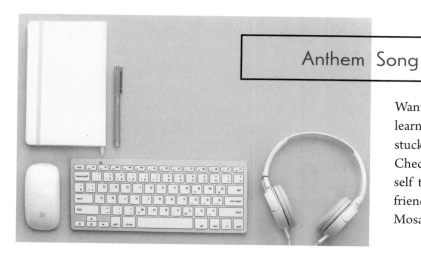

Anthem Song

Want to remember the truth you've learned today? A great way to get truth stuck in your head is through music. Check out this great song to remind yourself that Jesus is the most amazing best friend you could ever have: "Tremble" by Mosaic MSC.

Day 4: Letters from a Big God

Don't just take our word for it—your Creator has a lot to say on this subject. Here are a few verses you can check out to learn more about God's perspective. As you read, ask the Holy Spirit to point out an important verse for you and write it down in your journal, on your mirror, or on a post-it note you can put someplace where you'll see it every day.

John 10:14—15 and John 15:14—16

Day 5: Note to Self

Write a short note to yourself or God about the things you've learned from this chapter. What points really stood out to you? What do you want to remember as you go into this next week? How has this chapter changed your perspective about God or yourself?

Dear _____

YOU

belong

_____

chapter four

Dear little sister,

Do you have a favorite pair of jeans? That pair that makes you feel like a million bucks every time you slide them on? They're the go-to jeans that fit perfectly as if they were custom-made just for you.

Learning about yourself and your identity as a daughter can be like searching for the perfect pair of jeans. Sometimes you try on a few different styles in your teenage years. You might try on being the cool girl, or maybe the creative one. Or perhaps you explore being the wild child or the good student who gets the top marks.

I spent a lot of time as a teenager trying to figure out who I was. I searched for identity in places that couldn't give me what I was looking for. I tried to fit into the crowd by speaking, dressing, acting, and thinking like everyone else. The problem was, I wasn't like everyone else. I was, and still am, a unique child of God, fearfully and wonderfully made. I just didn't know it.

I guess I should back up and tell you the whole story about why understanding who I am was such a big deal for me.

When I was born, my birth parents weren't able to take care of me. I was adopted into a wonderful family. Whenever my adoption story was told to me as a child, it was the following beautiful version. My adoptive parents told me that they had two boys and wanted a baby girl to make their family complete. So they went to the baby store that had a whole bunch of cute little babies all lined up ready for their forever families. Up and down the aisles they went to pick out the perfect little girl. When they came to me, my mom said they just knew I was the one they loved. Suddenly I belonged. I was their daughter.

In my mind, I imagined my parents shopping with a little cart, picking me out from a line-up of babies on a shelf. I knew the story wasn't true, but what imprinted on my young mind was that I was wanted. Out of all the babies, my parents chose me because I was perfect.

Just telling this story puts a smile on my face. I hear my parents say, "You are loved. You belong to us."

Sometimes in your life, the truth you know will get exchanged for a lie. I don't know when it happened exactly, but over time I started to develop a different story in my head about being adopted. I started to think I was unwanted. I believed that somehow I wasn't good enough. Instead of feeling treasured and loved, I started to feel rejected and unlovable. I started to feel insecure, like somehow I'd lost a bit of myself I could never get back. I wondered, "Who am I?" But the answers I heard in my head were all lies.

I was faulty. I was a troublemaker. I was unloved.

Because of this broken way of thinking, I kind of lost myself. Believing I was unlovable, I tried on being the bad girl and found I was pretty good at it. I even became the black sheep of the family, the one that was different, in trouble, and not like my perfect white sheep brothers.

Really, I felt like a lost sheep.

Luke 15:4–6 says,

Suppose one of you has a hundred sheep and loses one of them. Doesn't he leave the ninety-nine in the open country and go after the lost sheep until he finds it? And when he finds it, he joyfully puts it on his shoulders and goes home. Then he calls his friends and neighbors together and says, "Rejoice with me; I have found my lost sheep." (NIV)

Our Good Shepard doesn't leave us lost. He goes out looking for the ones who have forgotten who they belong to and reminds us that our true identity is found in Him. He pursues those who have lost their way and don't know who they are. He goes after them because of His great love. He goes wherever they have wandered. No distance is too far. He picks them up, puts them on His shoulders, and says, "This one is mine. She belongs to me." He then tells everyone who will listen, "This is my daughter."

I want to tell you something really important, a truth that I've learned. I want you to know it as you're exploring the question of your identity. Hopefully it will save you from the painful struggle and wandering that happens to sheep who have forgotten who they belong to.

Only the love of God can tell you who you are. It's the answer to your heart's cry. You're loved because you belong to Him. You were adopted by God, which means you're His daughter, created in His likeness. You're the joy of your Creator. You are His chosen one. Because of His love, you are in the family of God. You are a daughter.

Sister, that's my story. It's who I am. I'm not the black sheep anymore. I've thrown away that ill-fitting pair of jeans and found the perfect fit. I'm a daughter of God. As a beloved daughter, I'm carried on the shoulders of my Father, and so are you, little sister.

Love,

Shezza Ansloos

Thoughts from Heather

Maybe you can relate to Sherry's story because you were also adopted. But even if you weren't adopted in the natural, you were adopted in the Spirit when you chose to follow Jesus. So what does it mean to be adopted as a child of God and what difference does it really make in your life? We're going to have a look at what adoption meant in New Testament times to get a better understanding of how significant it is that God has adopted us into His family.

Romans 8:15 says, *"The Spirit you received does not make you slaves, so that you live in fear again; rather, the Spirit you received brought about your adoption to sonship. And by him we cry, 'Abba, Father'"* (NIV).

When Paul wrote the book of Romans, adoption wasn't common among the Jewish people, but it was practiced among the Greeks and Romans. So when the early church read these words, they would have understood them in the context of Roman adoption practices and laws. Children weren't adopted just so they could have a family after being given up by their own. Rather, they were adopted so that the adoptive parents could pass on their inheritance to the adopted child. In some cases, families would even adopt one of their own slaves, freeing that slave and giving them immediate inheritance and ownership in the family. So when Paul writes about not receiving the spirit of slavery but instead the spirit of adoption, this is exactly what he's talking about.

What does this mean for you? It means you didn't just go from a slave to a free person when you accepted Jesus. You went from being a slave to being a daughter, and gained access to an inheritance as well!

Romans 8:17 says, *"Now if we are children, then we are heirs—heirs of God and co-heirs with Christ, if indeed we share in his sufferings in order that we may also share in his glory"* (NIV).

According to today's law, children don't become heirs until their parents or grandparents die. Paul's metaphor of adoption doesn't make as much sense in our day because we can't be God's heirs without God's death. But in Roman law, all the members of a family had joint ownership of their property. All children of any age, natural or adopted, were already heirs while their father lived and had joint control of the family's assets. This is the

legal background to what Paul is saying. In other words, it is birth, not death, that gives a child her inheritance. As soon as a child was legally adopted by her parents, she also had access and control of her inheritance.

The same is true for us as adopted daughters of God. The moment we said yes to Him and He said yes to us, we became daughters with legal access to all the resources of our Father. That means whatever Jesus (our adopted brother) has access to, we have access to. The power to heal the sick, cast out demons, share the gospel, perform miracles—everything that Jesus did—we can do too! I know it sounds crazy, but that's exactly what these verses in Romans 8 are saying.

If this is true, then adoption isn't just about us belonging to a family, it's also about our response and *responsibility* as daughters with access to an inheritance. We are no longer slaves who just do what they are told. We are daughters of a King, which makes us princesses. This means we have a responsibility to the people we interact with every day. We are a representation of our King and His Kingdom to the world around us.

I know that's a lot of information to take in, but let me just break it down to the basics for you.

Before Christ, we were *slaves* to sin.

After we said yes to Jesus, we were *adopted* into God's family as daughters.

Our adoption gives us *belonging*.

Our adoption also gives us an *inheritance*.

We are *chosen*, *accepted*, and we have a *responsibility* to steward what we've been given.

Our Response

Sherry said in her letter that understanding she was a daughter of God changed her life and gave her a new identity. Instead of being defined by whether her natural parents were able to care for her, or whether she was well-liked by her peers, she found security in knowing that God had come and found her when she was like a lost sheep. He chose her. He pursued her. He called her His own.

I hope you're beginning to see that all the same things are true about you. Regardless of how loved and accepted you feel by your family and peers, regardless of the kind of lifestyle you've been living or the mistakes you've made, the Good Shepherd is always pursuing you. I hope this truth sinks deep into your heart and rewrites the story you've been telling yourself.

But I also hope it doesn't stop there. I hope you don't just get this truth and allow it to change you. I hope and pray you can pass it on to those around you. I hope you can see the incredible inheritance you've been given and use it to generously give to others.

Love always,

Heather

My Prayer for You

Father, thank You for this sister of mine. Thank You that we get to be part of the same family because You adopted us and called us Your own. Not because You felt bad for us, but because You chose us. Bless my sister to know that she is chosen by You. Even if she doesn't feel seen and loved by her family or in her group of friends, remind her that she is Your special one. She is Your heir and co-heirs with Christ. May this knowledge encourage her to reach out and share that love and acceptance with the people in her community. Amen.

Soul Selfie

I feel loved when...

Day 1: Bullet Journaling

Use the prompt "I feel loved when …" and jot down your ideas in point form. No need for full sentences or perfect handwriting. Pull out some colored pens or pencils and get messy!

Day 2: Live the Letter

Pencil It In (small step)

Make a list of the things you've inherited because of the family you're in. Maybe it's resources like time, money, or education. Or maybe it's a strong sense of identity, belonging, or confidence. Thank God for that inheritance and try not to take it for granted.

Put It In Ink (bigger step)

Think of one way you can share that inheritance with someone else this week. Donate time or money to a local program that connects to your heart, reach out to someone who's lonely instead of just hanging with your regular crew, encourage someone who's feeling insecure, etc. Write down how it made you feel to share this inheritance with your community.

Day 3: Reflection

1. What's one way you've felt rejected, like you didn't belong?

_____

_____

2. How does knowing that you were adopted into God's family make you feel, and why?

_____

_____

3. How does knowing you have access to all the resources of heaven impact the way you live your life?

_____

_____

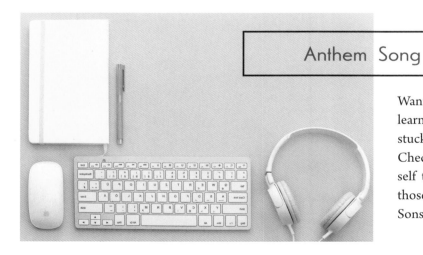

Anthem Song

Want to remember the truth you've learned today? A great way to get truth stuck in your head is through music. Check out this great song to remind yourself that you can be real with God and those around you: "Rest in You" by All Sons & Daughters.

Day 4: Letters from a Big God

Don't just take our word for it—your Creator has a lot to say on this subject. Here are a few verses you can check out to learn more about God's perspective. As you read, ask the Holy Spirit to point out an important verse for you and write it down in your journal, on your mirror, or on a post-it note you can put someplace where you'll see it every day.

Romans 15:7, Matthew 28:19, Ephesians 2:8—9

Day 5: Note to Self

Write a short note to yourself or God about the things you've learned from this chapter. What points really stood out to you? What do you want to remember as you go into this next week? How has this chapter changed your perspective about God or yourself?

Dear _____

YOU ARE

incomparable

_____

chapter five ⚡

Dear sister,

Comparison is a killer—a killer of hopes, dreams, and relationships. One of my mentors used to tell me, "Sometimes you lose when you compare yourself to others, but even worse, sometimes you win."

I used to struggle with comparison and intimidation on a daily basis, to the point that I was so scared to speak in most social situations. It normally happened when I sized up my competition and felt that sinking feeling that I'd lost, that they were better, prettier, funnier, or more interesting than me. It made me feel empty, like I had nothing to offer, so I closed myself off from people. After all, you can't be rejected when people can't see you, right?

But on occasion I would look at my competition and I'd win. I'd be the most talkative in that circle of friends, afraid of nothing and seemingly carefree. I must have sounded so noisy and clanging to heaven in these times because there wasn't much love in my heart and I surely hadn't learned to love myself yet. In those moments, I only felt worthy because I felt better than someone else, and that's not true worth.

After years of this cycle of comparison, I was confronted with the fact that even though I was surrounded by people, I felt alone. In sheltering myself from rejection, I had also barricaded myself from love and the possibility of true friendship. I had some acquaintances and a family who loved me, but no one knew the true me. My problem with comparison led me straight into a life of loneliness.

Have you ever been there? Are you there right now, playing the comparison game and coming up short? Or even worse, do you find your value in being better than everyone around you? I'm here to tell you, sister, that there's another way to live. There's a way to find true value in who God made you to be and, as a result, experience deep connection with the people around you.

For me, it started with the Holy Spirit taking me on a journey to get to know myself. Comparison is only an issue when you don't know or love who you are. I started small by writing things down about myself that I thought were beautiful. I started letting my opinions take shape and speaking them out instead of claiming I had none. Sometimes it was something as simple as saying why I liked a certain flavor of gum. Other times it was about speaking out on an important issue. I got to know myself more and more until I saw a real, raw, beautiful human taking shape. It turned out that I was marvelous—full of interesting thoughts, opinions, likes and dislikes, emotions, and jokes—so many jokes. I was actually pretty hilarious.

I realized that I'd never taken the time to see who God had created me to be. I had only given value to what I could do and what I could do better than others. I hadn't paid attention to who I really was on the inside. I reacted to my environment rather than shaping it with my God-given awesomeness. There's a reason the Bible says we should love our neighbors as ourselves. You can only love others to the extent that you love yourself, and you can only receive love to the extent that you love yourself.

So knowing and understanding who you are is very important. From the surface level stuff to the depths of your heart, every part is important.

I walked around for far too long without true, deep connection, and I want so much more for you. But connection isn't made when we're honest only with ourselves. We need to be honest and open with the people around us too. You have an amazing personality, a unique sense of humor, and a combination of likes and dislikes that hasn't been seen by this world in anyone before you. In order to form true connections, you need to show these parts of yourself to the world—your mess and strength, your darkness and light.

I want you to have the freedom that comes through learning to love—first loving yourself and then loving those around you. The more accurately you see yourself, the more you can share who you are with those around you. I want you to see how valuable you are and how you were designed to positively impact the world. All you need to do is open up the steel doors you've been living behind and start letting people in. Don't hold back out of fear, because you can always overcome fear with love.

Comparison is a trap, like a hamster wheel that keeps us running and running but going nowhere. The first step is to recognize this trap, choose to get off the wheel, and determine to find a better way to live. I want who we truly are to flow out of our lives like a powerful river, without any rocks or obstacles in the way. I want us to be fearless and fully content with who God created us to be. I want that for myself, and more than anything, sweet sister, I want that for you.

Much love,

Kristene DiMarco

Thoughts from Heather

So often when we think about comparison, we think about all the ways in which we aren't as amazing as those around us. For me, it only takes a minute or two on Instagram to feel the way Kristene described—like I don't measure up. I'm not as stylish or beautiful or adventurous or even as spiritual as all the girls I see in my feed. But the truth is, this kind of thinking is a trap. Even the girls who seem to have it all together, with thousands of likes, comments, and followers, feel this way sometimes. It's time to stop playing the comparison game and replace comparison and competition with connection.

This isn't a new problem. This is a challenge young women have been facing since the beginning of time—all the way back to Eve in the garden, actually.

You might be thinking, *But who did Eve have to compare herself to?* Well, it wasn't that she had other beautiful women to measure herself up against, but she was told the first lie a woman has ever been told—the same lie that causes us to compare ourselves to and compete with others.

> *The serpent told the Woman, "You won't die. God knows that the moment you eat from that tree, you'll see what's really going on. You'll be just like God, knowing everything, ranging all the way from good to evil."*
> —Genesis 3:4–5, MSG

The lie Eve was told that day was that she wasn't good enough, that there was something she could do to become better. The enemy told her that she could be just like God, but the truth is that she already was. She had been created in the image of God and didn't have to do anything to earn her value or identity. But how did Satan get her to eat the apple? By telling her that something was missing and it was her job to get it—that she had to *do* something to *be* someone.

Every time we *do* something to try and *be* someone, we live under the curse of the enemy.

I lived this way for most of my early teen years. I closely watched the girls around me and compared myself to them, carefully measuring myself against them. I particularly watched the ones who were most popular, thinking that somehow if I could change myself to become more like them, I could have what they had. But instead of making me more confident and popular, it seemed to have the opposite effect. Instead of being drawn to me, people didn't know who I was.

How do we free ourselves from comparison and competition? Kristene gave us some amazing tips in her letter and I want to dig a little deeper into some of her suggestions.

Get to Know You

How well do you know yourself? What are the things that fire you up and get you excited about life? What are your favorite ways to refuel when you're drained? These are the kinds of questions we don't have time to think about when we're constantly comparing ourselves to others. It makes me sad to think that instead of exploring our likes and dislikes, strengths and passions, we study the likes and dislikes, strengths and passions of other people. And because of social media, we often only see the bright side of everyone else's life. As a result, we end up comparing our worst days to the their best ones and constantly feel like we don't measure up.

What if we decided to take some of that time and instead spend it getting to know ourselves? What if we put our phones down for an hour and spend that time exploring a new hobby or doing something we love? Explore the wonder that is you and learn to love all those unique, quirky things about yourself. You might be surprised at what you discover.

Love You

As you spend more time getting to know yourself, accept the things you find and learn to love yourself. It's easy to think that loving God and others are the two most important things we are called to do. But the Bible says that we are to love our neighbors *as we love ourselves*. If we don't love ourselves, we can't really love our neighbors. If we're critical and judgmental of ourselves, we will be critical and judgmental of others. If we feel like we're never good enough, how can we really make someone else feel like they're good enough?

Sister, you can't give away what you don't have. So loving yourself is actually the least selfish thing you can do. Loving yourself is a gift to those around you.

The next time you discover something new about yourself, accept and celebrate it. Next time you receive a compliment, say thank you instead of brushing it off. And next time you're tempted to hide something about yourself that you see as a weakness, own it and invite others to add their strength to that area.

Celebrate Others

One of the best ways to combat comparison and competition is to celebrate the people around you, especially the ones you're tempted to be jealous of. Some call this "acting in the opposite spirit." All that means is that you choose to do the opposite of what you're feeling. So if you're feeling jealous and you want to pull away from someone, do the opposite. Go up to them, introduce yourself, and give them a genuine compliment. This action takes the power out of the ugly feeling you have and gives it to something good instead. It might feel like you're being fake at first, but you're actually acting out of faith.

You and I both know that jealousy is gross and not something we want in our lives. So instead of acting jealous when you feel jealous, *act* loving and you'll start to *feel* loving. Act generous and you'll start to feel generous. Act in faith for the feeling you want to have.

When you reach out to someone you feel intimidated by, you build connection instead of fostering comparison. Get to know the person behind the image they portray. What you'll find is that everyone has a story and no one is perfect. Even the girl who seems to have everything together has insecurities, quirks, and flaws. You might even find that the person you wish could be your best friend isn't who you thought they were—the image they portrayed doesn't quite line up with who they are up close and personal. No matter the outcome, it's always better to get to know someone and build connection before drawing conclusions about who they are and comparing yourself to the image you have of them.

So find ways to celebrate the other women in your life. Refuse to get sucked into the black hole of comparison and choose to use your energy and words to build others up. You can definitely lose when you act out of jealousy and competition, but you never lose when you act out of love.

Love always,

Heather

My Prayer for You

God, I break the lies my sweet sister has believed—that she is less than in comparison to other girls. We say no to competition and comparison and the way it is trying to rob her of her true identity and strength as Your daughter. We agree with the truth that You made her uniquely and she has something to offer the world that no one else can. Protect her heart and mind from believing that she is anything less than Your precious daughter because her life doesn't look like someone else's. Help her to agree with the truth that she is full of beauty and purpose. Amen.

Soul Selfie

10 facts about me

Day 1: Bullet Journaling

Use the prompt "10 Facts about Me" and jot down your ideas in point form. No need for full sentences or perfect handwriting. Pull out some colored pens or pencils and get messy!

Day 2: Live the Letter

Pencil It In (small step)

One of the best ways to combat comparison and competition is to celebrate others. This week, reach out to one person you really admire but feel too shy or inadequate to talk to. Write a note, email, or talk face to face and tell them one thing you admire about them. Before you reach out, ask God how He sees them and feel free to encourage them with what He tells you.

Put It In Ink (bigger step)

The next time you find yourself discouraged because you've been comparing yourself to someone else, reach out and tell a friend. Resist the urge to try and deal with this struggle on your own. We were made to walk through these challenges in community. Find someone who will remind you of the truth and won't join in your pity party.

Day 3: Reflection (fill in the blanks)

My favorites: _____

_____

My strengths: _____

_____

My weaknesses: _____

_____

My dreams: _____

_____

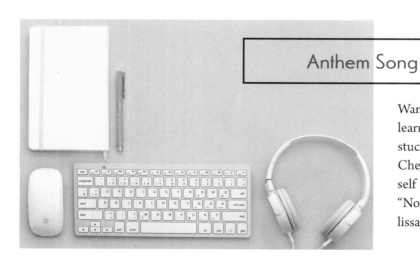

Anthem Song

Want to remember the truth you've learned today? A great way to get truth stuck in your head is through music. Check out this great song to remind yourself of your incomparable value to God: "No Longer Slaves" by Jonathan and Melissa Helser.

Day 4: Letters from a Big God

Don't just take our word for it—your Creator has a lot to say on this subject. Here are a few verses you can check out to learn more about God's perspective. As you read, ask the Holy Spirit to point out an important verse for you and write it down in your journal, on your mirror, or on a post-it note you can put someplace where you'll see it every day.

Galatians 1:10, 2 Corinthians 12:10—18

Day 5: Note to Self

Write a short note to yourself or God about the things you've learned from this chapter. What points really stood out to you? What do you want to remember as you go into this next week? How has this chapter changed your perspective about God or yourself?

Dear _____

YOU DO

chapter six

Dear Sister,

I didn't have my first boyfriend until I was twenty-four years old. This meant that I was date-less and boyfriend-less in high school *and* college. I remember telling my mom, "Nobody likes me." She would encourage me, saying, "They're just intimated by you, Tiff." I didn't know if that meant I was big-boned, had too much arm hair, or was just scary to look at, but I knew she was just trying to make me feel better.

Before I got married, I spent a lot of time looking around and thinking to myself, "Is that him? Is that him? Or is *that* him?" I was always curious about who I was going to marry. Looking back, I realize it used up way more space in my brain than it needed to. All I really needed to do was pay attention to whoever and whatever was right in front of me, live my life, and let everything else fall into place. So often, we as girls want to make a relationship happen and have it look like the movies, but trust me, you don't really want what's in the movies even though it might seem exciting and perfect at first glance.

Another thing I struggled with as a teenager was my weight, meaning that I struggled with *thinking* I was heavy, which also fueled this lie: "No one likes me because I'm fat." I remember looking back at photos of myself in a swimsuit a few years after high school and thinking, "Wow, I was skinny." But that's definitely not how I felt at the time. I thought I wasn't skinny because there were girls who were skinnier. I carried that for years. In fact, I still have to fight it off now, and I'm married to an amazing man who loves God and is *hot*. Still, it's funny how those lies want to stick to you and continue to try to steal, kill, and destroy.

If there's any advice I can give you, little sis, it's this: stop comparing yourself to others. Stop looking at other girls and thinking, "I'm not as pretty as her or I'm not as skinny as her." The truth is that this is all nonsense. You were fearfully and wonderfully made by a Creator who makes no mistakes. He fashioned you with your eyes, skin, dimples, and personality for a reason and a purpose. The sooner you can embrace the real you, the you that God created, the sooner you'll live more fully alive and on purpose. This freedom will also allow you to champion other girls and cheer them on.

Make a careful exploration of who you are and the work you have been given, and then sink yourself into that. Don't be impressed with yourself. Don't compare yourself with others. Each of you must take responsibility for doing the creative best you can with your own life.

—Galatians 6:4–5, MSG

If I could go back to my teenage self and tell young Tiff any bit of advice, it would be this: "Girl, you need to do a lot less looking and whole lot more living." This is your season to grow, bloom, and work on yourself. This is *your* season, girl. Don't miss it or try to bypass it.

When my dad unexpectedly passed a few years ago, the idea of living vs. looking became so much more real and urgent to me. I realized that we never know when our time is up. Therefore, it's important to just enjoy everything in front of you, love the people God has put in your life, and simply be thankful because things could change tomorrow.

My dad did exactly that. I saw him the day before he passed away, not knowing it would be the last time I would hug him, talk with him, and laugh with him. However, he lived so fully and joyfully that I have no regrets even though we didn't get to say goodbye. He lived with joy, freely loved others, and consistently made others smile simply by being himself. Thankfully, I have the hope of heaven and I know we'll see each other again.

God chose you to live in your town, have your look, have your passions, attend your school, have your sense of humor, have your quirks, and have your dreams. And He placed you into your family for such a time as this.

Don't waste your time wishing you had someone else's life. Embrace what God has given you. Chances are He gave you more than you realize. Use what you've been given to be a light. Use it for His glory. Use it for good. Use it to change your world and bloom right where He planted you. There's only one you… and no one can compare to that.

Your big sis,

Tiffany Thurston

Thoughts from Heather

I love the idea Tiffany shared about doing less looking and more living. This is such a powerful idea, isn't it? We spend so much time looking at everyone else's lives that we end up missing our own.

Here are some of the things Tiffany suggested we look at less often:

- other girls—such as their size, strengths, and talents.
- which guy we're gonna end up marrying.
- the way other people are living their lives.

Here's what I'd add to that list. Let's look less at:

- our phones.
- other people's Instagram feeds.
- the things we don't like about ourselves.
- the next stage of our lives, whether it's marriage, children, a future job, etc.

It's okay to think and even dream about these things from time to time, but let's not obsess about them so much that we miss out on the people and opportunities right in front of us.

Here's how Tiffany described what "more living" looks like:

- embrace the way God made you.
- pay attention to the people right in front of you and cheer them on.
- be thankful for what you've been given.

What would you add to that list? What does it look like for you to do less looking and more living right where you are?

For me, "more living" looks like:

- more laughter, even if it means laughing at myself.
- not caring so much what people think about me.
- going on adventures and trying new things.
- giving people compliments, encouragement, and gifts like they're going out of style.

I want to live life to the fullest, just like Tiffany's dad did. I don't want to have any regrets. I don't want to waste my time and energy looking at and comparing myself to other people and the lives they're living.

Sister, your life is a beautiful gift and today is twenty-four hours you'll never get back. Don't miss it because you have your eyes glued to a screen full of edited images of someone else's adventures. Don't miss it because you're waiting for life to come and happen to you. It's happening right now! Don't miss it because you're focused on a past you can't change, no matter how hard you try.

All you have is today.

Matthew 6:33–34 says it like this:

Steep your life in God-reality, God-initiative, God-provisions. Don't worry about missing out. You'll find all your everyday human concerns will be met.

Give your entire attention to what God is doing right now, and don't get worked up about what may or may not happen tomorrow. God will help you deal with whatever hard things come up when the time comes. (MSG)

This passage gives us some great instructions about how to do less looking and more living.

1. Steep your life in God-reality. I love this one because it reminds me of one of my favorite things to do: drink tea. When you steep a tea bag in hot water, the water takes on the flavor of the tea and becomes something totally different. It's no longer water, it's delicious tea. And this process of steeping takes time and heat.

The same process occurs when we steep ourselves in God-reality. When we try to think the way He thinks and act the way He acts, we become more like Him. The more time we spend in His Word and soaking in His presence, the more we are changed into something new. Sometimes it takes a little heat to refine us into the person

He's created us to be. The challenges we face aren't always from God, but He does use them to grow character in us and prepare us for the good things He has in store for us.

2. Don't worry about missing out. This is a tough one. I mean, who doesn't struggle with FOMO—the fear of missing out? But here's the truth, sister. When you live with the fear of missing out, that very fear causes you to miss out! You miss out on the person or opportunity right in front of you. That person could actually be the one to help you get where you're wanting to go, but if you're just wishing you were with someone else, you might miss it.

God is looking for people He can trust, people who aren't worried about being the most popular, influential, or sought after. He's looking for people who will be faithful with the little things. FOMO distracts you from becoming that person.

3. Look for what God is doing right now. It's so easy to ask why. Why are things the way they are? Why do I have to wait? Why can't I have what that girl has?

But why isn't a helpful question, because you're probably never going to get the answer. A better question you can ask is what. What are you doing, God, and how can I partner with you?

The truth is that God is always doing something. If you can bring yourself into the present moment and figure out what He's doing, you can be part of the action! When you're in tune with what God is doing, there's no way you can be missing out.

Sister, let's not get worked up about what will or won't happen tomorrow. Let's trust that we are exactly where we are supposed to be, not because of who is there with us but because God is there with us. Let's be the kind of people who embrace the gift of right now by doing less looking and more living. Let's squeeze every bit of goodness out of this moment, this day, this time we've been given.

Love always,

Heather

My Prayer for You

God I thank You for the gift of life you've given my sister. Help her not to miss the beautiful way You are working because she is distracted with looking everywhere else. Teach her what it means to do less looking and more living. Remind her often of the goodness and beauty right in front of her. Amen.

Soul Selfie

less looking, more living

Day 1: Bullet Journaling

Use the prompt "Less looking, more living" and jot down your ideas in point form. No need for full sentences or perfect handwriting. Pull out some colored pens or pencils and get messy!

Day 2: Live the Letter

Pencil It In (small step)

Spend the day looking for the way God is working. Try to pay attention to the people He's putting in your path and the way His Spirit is leading you. Set an alarm on your phone to go off every hour to remind yourself to look for what He is doing and listen to what He is saying.

Put It In Ink (bigger step)

Instead of just doing this for one day, commit to doing it all week. Every time you find yourself asking why, change it to what. What are you doing, God, and how can I partner with you? Write down what you observe and then share it with someone at the end of the week.

Day 3: Reflection

1. What do you want to do less of in your life right now?

_____

_____

2. What do you want more of in your life?

_____

_____

3. How do you feel when you spend your time looking at other people's lives instead of living your

own? _____

_____

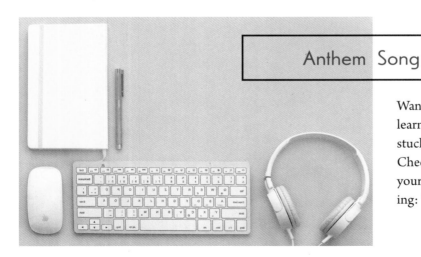

Anthem Song

Want to remember the truth you've learned today? A great way to get truth stuck in your head is through music. Check out these great songs to remind yourself to do less looking and more living: "Wonder" by Hillsong United.

Day 4: Letters from a Big God

Don't just take our word for it—your Creator has a lot to say on this subject. Here are a few verses you can check out to learn more about God's perspective. As you read, ask the Holy Spirit to point out an important verse for you and write it down in your journal, on your mirror, or on a post-it note you can put someplace where you'll see it every day.

Galatians 5:25—26, Colossians 3: 1—3

Day 5: Note to Self

Write a short note to yourself or God about the things you've learned from this chapter. What points really stood out to you? What do you want to remember as you go into this next week? How has this chapter changed your perspective about God or yourself?

Dear _____

YOU ARE

complete

_____

chapter seven

Dear sweet sister,

Boys were never really my thing. Growing up, I was just one of the guys, competing in obstacle courses and dressing in Nike tracksuits, hoping my breasts would never develop so I would always fit in with the crowd. It was a man's world on my street. Not beating them meant I had to join them. But never with the power of seduction, oh no.

Romance with such a species didn't make any sense to me. I didn't understand boys at all. Why, for example, did they need to physically fight instead of smoothing things out with their words and a cup of milk? What was so great about GI Joe when you could have an EZ Bake Oven that made a *ding* sound when it was done? I played the Three Musketeers with them every dinnertime with plastic swords and that's about as much physical and emotional contact I planned to have with them. I didn't want to be rescued from a fire-breathing dragon by a blond-haired stranger. I wanted to learn sword-fighting myself.

I was happy to be one of the boys, but I definitely didn't want to actually date them, or think about kissing them.

Until one morning I woke up, a fifteen-year-old girl, and boys became magnetic. All of a sudden I was saying yes, yes, and yes again to any boy who asked me out. Dating at this age wasn't exactly meaningful, but I do remember the profound effect these guys had on me.

I became a hopeless romantic overnight, and for many years I found my value in the affection of boys. I used their attention like a drug to calm some pain in me, thinking it would satisfy my thirst for love and acceptance. At times it did, but it was so fleeting, and because I didn't recognize the motivation behind why I was dating, or who I was dating, I gained a back-catalogue of poorly chosen guys. Guys who had substances issues, guys who couldn't commit, guys who were critical, guys who would tell me it was between me or another girl, guys who couldn't handle themselves on physical or emotional levels.

The more pain I experienced, the more I needed another story to prove the last relationship wrong, to prove that it wasn't my fault and that I definitely hadn't asked for this. And truly, I hadn't. But so easily I fell for the charm. From there, like a sickness, my people-pleasing, my desire to be loved by guys, overtook my love for myself, my self-worth, and my identity.

In the book of Matthew, Christ says, *"Man shall not live on bread alone, but on every word that comes from the mouth of God"* (Matthew 4:4, NIV). I was living by man alone. Oh how I wish I had listened to these words of truth then. How I wish I'd taken more time to find out how God saw me, how precious I was in His eyes, how God's love confirmed my identity, not the love of another human being.

There was always something in the back of my mind telling me this wasn't the best way, going from guy to guy, but my co-dependent needs were stronger than my logic. I had a need to be seen, to be valued, to be known. If I had started with the value God had for me, I'd have valued myself.

It took counsel, a humble heart, and a brutally honest father to tell me that I wasn't valuing myself. It took the Lord to show me that no princess who knows her worth would settle for what I had settled for. No young woman of hope and dignity would allow this behavior to continue. They would leave these guys behind.

But I stayed in unhealthy relationships because of fear, a hope they would change, or a hope I would change. But none of them were right and I wasted too much time trying to be something for them without ever discovering me, who I was and what I wanted.

So the cleanse began—something I should have done at the end of my teens. I left the string of guys behind to explore my dreams, my faults, my love for theatre, my dislike for empty charm, and my love of humor without the need for it to replace intelligence. I started looking for a rested man, one who was comfortable and who spoke with kindness and respect. I wanted a guy who wouldn't rush me, or over-promise or move on to the next best thing within a week. I was no longer willing to compromise.

My sweet sister, may my pain be your gain. Start within, by knowing that you are worthy of great kindness. Be authentic with what you see in the mirror, but never with a critical voice. Crush denial and stop blaming others. Take ownership of who you are and start asking what makes you, you. If there are immature and disrespectful guys in your life, cut the cord and wish them a pleasant day. Don't hang onto feelings towards guys who probably aren't thinking much about your heart. Don't let their comments define who you are. If they don't value you now, they probably never will. Don't whisper sweet nothings to strangers who haven't earned your trust yet. Don't let your purity be compromised for the sake of a quick fix. You're fighting for long-term gain— intimacy, growth, love, and holiness.

Remember, we don't attract who we are, we attract what we believe we are worth. Sister, you are worth the fight.

Xoxo

Your big sis,

Carrie Lloyd

Thoughts from Heather

Relationships with guys are *complicated*. They take up so much of our time and energy that could be spent on things that are way more fun, and way less stressful. But Carrie offers some great advice and wisdom about how to approach dating in a healthy way.

The biggest key Carrie shared is to not base your identity in the way guys treat you. I wish I would have understood this simple truth when I was sixteen. If they paid attention to me I felt important and beautiful, and if they ignored me I felt unattractive and undesirable. It's so silly now, because from what I know about teen boys they have absolutely no idea about the effect they have on us girls! We read way too much into how they act, but they aren't thinking about it at all.

The best way to save ourselves from being so affected by guys and their opinions of us is to root our identity in who God says we are.

Even though I cared a lot about what the boys I liked thought of me, I had the benefit of growing up in a family where I was told all the time how much God loved me. My gifts and passions were recognized and encouraged by my family and friends and I knew I was valuable and worthy of love. This foundation saved me from a lot of bad decisions.

But maybe you didn't have that kind of experience growing up and maybe you're struggling to believe you are deserving of the most extravagant love.

If that's you, can I challenge you with something?

Stop dating.

I know, I know, it sounds extreme, but if you really don't know how beautiful and smart and gifted you are and find yourself constantly waiting for a cute boy to tell you those things, or give you that love, it's time to take a step back. You may even need to end the relationship you're in right now because too much of your identity is wrapped up in the person you're with. Take some time to be single so that you can learn to let God love you *and*

learn to love yourself. Most likely you're going to spend the majority of your life married to a man, so why not take some time right now to learn how to be happy and settled without needing that affirmation?

If you're not dating but still spending most of your time wishing you were, stop that too! The truth is that if you're unhappy by yourself, eventually you're going to be unhappy dating that hot guy you're daydreaming about. If you feel like you aren't worthy of being loved, that isn't going to change even when you're in an amazing relationship. You take your insecurities wherever you go. And unfortunately, if you don't love yourself and know your worth, it's likely that you'll compromise your standards and allow yourself to be mistreated way more easily than if you were confident of your value.

You might be wondering to yourself, "So what am I supposed to do when I'm by myself?"

Find somewhere quiet and ask God this question: "What do you love about me?" Ask it sincerely and listen for His response. Don't take out your phone or distract yourself with Netflix. Just sit for a few minutes—two whole minutes—and wait. Allow God to whisper His affection over you. Wait for Him to remind you of how He sees you. Sit in the satisfaction of His love and acceptance of you, just the way you are. Do this regularly—at least once a week. There's so much He wants to tell you if you'll only take the time to ask and listen.

Get in the Word. The Bible is full of powerful truth about who you are as a creation, daughter, and follower of God. Take some time to look for scriptures about who you are in Christ and what you have access to as a daughter of God. Find a good concordance (there are many online) and look up words and phrases like "daughter," "child of God," "inheritance," "co-heir," and read all about your true value from God's perspective. Pray and ask the Holy Spirit to reveal the truth in His Word so it can be planted like seeds in your heart and grow good fruit in your life.

When you do start dating, do it from a place of worthiness. I'm not talking perfection—but have a solid understanding of who you are as a daughter of God, what He thinks about you, and what you think about yourself.

Try not to let the guy you're dating replace God in your life. I know it's hard because he's right there and you can hear his voice and feel his hand in yours. But keep your relationship with God a priority, and by priority I mean that you actually set aside minutes in your day to sit with Him, ask Him questions, listen for His answers, and read His Word. It's so easy to get swept up in a romance and forget all about your first love.

If the guy you're dating starts treating you unkindly, or seems to lose interest, please don't do what I did. Don't change yourself to try to keep his attention. Don't compromise your standards because you think it'll make him stick around. And please don't stay even when everything inside you is telling you to let go.

Don't stay because of shame. Maybe you compromised your purity standards. Maybe you feel like damaged goods. But staying because of shame is never going to right the wrongs of your relationship. It's only going to take you deeper into something that will ultimately hurt you.

Don't stay hoping for him to change. People show you who they are over time. If this dude continues to show you that he's disrespectful, self-centered, or unable to follow through on his word, that likely isn't going to change. Pay attention to the way he treats his family, especially his mom, and don't ignore the warning signs just because he's a good kisser.

Don't stay because you're afraid of being alone. Trust me when I say that being alone, or even heartbroken, is so much better than being in a toxic relationship. Yes, it's hard to see all your friends coupling off, but being deeply entangled with the wrong person will feel way worse than loneliness does.

Sister, you deserve an incredible love and it will be totally worth the wait. So take the time now to invest in yourself and understanding who you are as God's daughter. Don't rush into something you're not sure about just because you don't want to be alone. Wait for the kind of guy who will treat you like the treasure you are.

Love always,

Heather

My Prayer for You

God, You know the person my sister will marry one day. Thank You for working on her behalf right now to get him ready to be an incredible husband for her. And thank You for getting her ready to be an amazing wife. I pray that she will have the patience to not rush ahead into a relationship that isn't from You. Help her to find her security in Your love, not the love of a boy. May she have the courage to make the hard decisions she needs to in order to protect her heart and stay close to You. Amen.

Soul Selfie

my dream guy

Day 1: Bullet Journaling

Use the prompt "My Dream Guy" and jot down your ideas in point form. No need for full sentences or perfect handwriting. Pull out some colored pens or pencils and get messy!

Day 2: Live the Letter

Pencil It In (small step)

On a scale from one to ten, how much would you say you love and accept yourself right now?

1—2—3—4—5—6—7—8—9—10

Write out why you chose this number:

Put It In Ink (bigger step)

Based on the number you chose, what's one thing about yourself that you can't change but can learn to accept? (It could be a physical feature, personality trait, etc.) What's one thing you can change? (Such as a habit you'd like to quit/start, a belief you'd like to change, etc.) Write down a step you can take this week to (1) accept what you can't change and (2) grow in the area you can change.

Day 3: Reflection

1. How do you feel about relationships with the opposite gender?

_____

_____

2. What's your biggest fear about dating/not dating and why?

_____

_____

3. What's one must-have quality you're looking for in a guy and why?

_____

_____

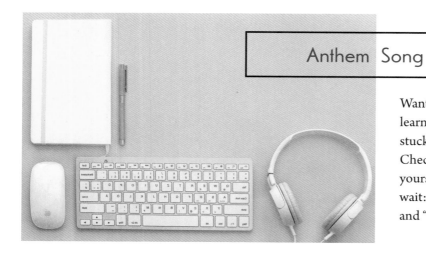

Anthem Song

Want to remember the truth you've learned today? A great way to get truth stuck in your head is through music. Check out these great songs to remind yourself that the right guy is worth the wait: "While I'm Waiting" by John Waller and "God Gave Me You" by Dave Barnes.

Day 4: Letters from a Big God

Don't just take our word for it—your Creator has a lot to say on this subject. Here are a few verses you can check out to learn more about God's perspective. As you read, ask the Holy Spirit to point out an important verse for you and write it down in your journal, on your mirror, or on a post-it note you can put someplace where you'll see it every day.

2 Corinthians 6:14—18

Day 5: Note to Self

Write a short note to yourself or God about the things you've learned from this chapter. What points really stood out to you? What do you want to remember as you go into this next week? How has this chapter changed your perspective about God or yourself?

Dear _____

YOUR INNER

world

_____

chapter eight

Dear Sister,

I grew up in a great family with two awesome parents who loved me very much. I had a happy childhood and nothing to complain about… until middle school. Ugh. I felt so small on the first day of sixth grade, a tiny nobody in a sea of unfamiliar faces.

I decided to try out for the cheerleading squad because I was desperate to find a place to belong, and all of the popular girls were trying out. They got lots of attention from the cute boys, probably because they had hit puberty a solid two years before me. They had boobs and bubbly personalities and seemed so confident. I hoped that if I could somehow be around them, maybe, just maybe, my boobs would grow and all that confidence would rub off on me.

I remember sobbing uncontrollably on the way home after finding out I hadn't made the cut. I had never felt such sadness. My mom's attempts to console me didn't actually speak to the deep hurt in my heart. I decided she didn't understand me, no one did, and I'd have to figure it out on my own.

Within the first few months of school, so many horrifying things piled up. One of the cheerleaders asked me in front of an entire group of girls if I was anorexic, the boy I liked dumped me for someone else, and my pre-algebra teacher was so mean that I felt sick in her class.

If school wasn't bad enough, our town hosted a middle school dance on Friday nights, which was basically the worst idea ever. Hundreds of other insecure, hormonal teenagers gathered in a dark, poorly chaperoned room to gossip, dance, make out, and poke fun at the wallflowers.

By Christmas, I was a mess! I literally cried every day after school. Moody music and my pillow became my best friends, and I'd discovered masturbation as a way to bring myself comfort and temporarily relieve the pressure. I felt like I was dying on the inside.

At some point I made friends, grew into my body, and learned my way around junior high. The sting of sixth grade wore off, but the coping mechanisms I'd picked up for how to deal with pressure, stress, and pain didn't get unlearned until much later in life.

Imagine a bottle of water that weighs about twenty ounces. Not that heavy, right? But when it comes to stress, the weight doesn't matter. What matters is how long you hold it. If you hold it for a minute, no problem. If you hold it for an hour, you'll have an ache in your arm. If you hold it for a day, your arm will feel numb and paralyzed.

The stresses and worries of life are like that bottle of water. Think about them for a while and nothing happens. Think about them a little longer and they begin to hurt. Think about them all day long and you'll feel paralyzed, incapable of doing anything. That stress can lead to depression, compulsion, isolation, anxiety, exhaustion, and even physical pain.

Healthy stress management has everything to do with how you talk to yourself. Feelings like happiness, anger, sadness, frustration, and anxiety originate with a thought, and humans think in words. Have you ever stopped to ask yourself about your self-talk?

- We talk to ourselves at a rate of 150–300 words a minute.
- Seventy percent of those words are *negative.*
- Of those negative words, seventy percent are unconscious.
- Ninety-five percent of those unconscious words will be repeated in your head tomorrow.

No wonder so many of us struggle with stress and anxiety. Most of the thoughts you have in a day are negative, and those thoughts are creating your emotions. If we can learn to manage our thoughts, we can keep the stress we feel at a manageable level. So how do we do it?

There's no way to get rid of negative self-talk and become emotionally and mentally strong without getting rid of guilt, shame, and self-condemnation. Girl, it's time to stand up and let the beauty of who God made you to be speak for itself. No one is more powerful to change your situation than you are. The truth is, if you don't choose who you're going to be in this world and what kind of life you'll live, the world will choose for you and it won't be what you want. Negative self-talk, shame, and guilt thrive in the dark, so the key to breakthrough is to bring all of yourself into the light.

Your ability to step into freedom hinges on your ability to share your inner world with someone you trust, someone who can help you walk through it. Let's be honest, if you knew how to do it on your own, you would have already done it! You need a mentor, counsellor, or youth pastor to love you unconditionally and help move you forward.

My heart for you is that you'll learn to love your story, however challenging or painful it's been. God created you for greatness, and His heart for you is that you'll live in peace and freedom.

You, little sister, are worth it!

Love,

Lauren Vallotton

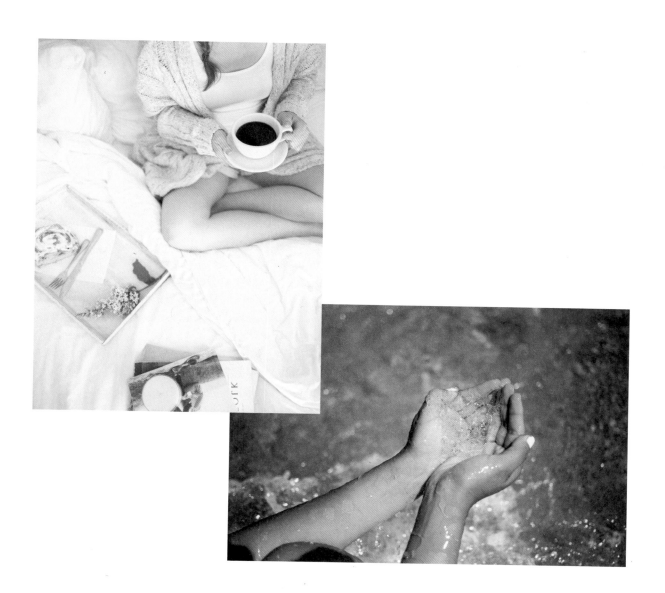

Thoughts from Heather

Isn't Lauren amazing? Her letter is so full of wisdom that you might need to go back and read it again. I'm so grateful for how honest she was about the challenges she faced as a teen and how she walked through them.

That analogy about carrying the bottle of water and how the longer you hold it, the heavier it gets—that's so powerful! The stress in your life, whether it's over something traumatic like loss or abuse or something as simple as feeling left out or overwhelmed by schoolwork, all feels heavy when you carry it on your own.

You weren't meant to do this life on your own. Yes, you always have God to lean on, but sometimes God will only bring you healing through other people. That's how much He wants us to be in healthy community.

Lauren briefly mentioned a few ways you can put your bottle down and deal with the stress in your life in a healthy way. We're going to take a closer look at some of her suggestions so you can feel equipped to take some practical steps to de-stress.

1. Get rid of the guilt, shame, and self-condemnation. These are some of the classic tools the enemy uses to try and get us down. He knows that if he can convince us we're unworthy of love, we'll stop trying to find freedom. And if he can convince us that we're the only ones struggling, we'll never share our struggle with others.

In order to walk forward in freedom, you need to confess your guilt, shame, and self-condemnation to God. When you tell Him all the things you're feeling guilty about and admit the negative thoughts you're having, you can experience His love and grace. 1 John 1:9 says, *"If we confess our sins, he is faithful and just and will forgive us our sins and purify us from all unrighteousness"* (NIV).

Maybe you didn't know that self-hatred was a sin, but anytime you have a thought in your head about yourself that isn't in God's head, you're calling Him a liar. That sounds a little harsh, but that's how dangerous it is to live with shame and self-hatred.

2. Bring it into the light. Lauren mentioned how important it is to share the things we're tempted to hide with trusted friends and counsellors. That secret you're keeping, bring it into the light. When you do, you'll find

that it's not nearly as bad as you thought it was. You'll discover that other people are struggling with the very same things and that you're not alone.

So find someone safe and be brutally honest with them about the pain you're feeling or the cycle you're caught in. Sister, you don't have to hide anymore. Come into the light and allow yourself to be fully seen and fully loved.

Proverbs 27:17 says, *"As iron sharpens iron, so one person sharpens another"* (NIV). We aren't weak for reaching out. We're actually stronger when we share our stress with someone who can help sharpen us.

3. Pay attention to your heart. It's so easy to just get swept away in the craziness of life and forget to pay attention to how our hearts are doing. We get so focused on how other people see us that sometimes we don't even see ourselves for who we really are.

One of the most powerful things I've learned in the last few years is to pay attention to my own heart. Notice when your mood switches quickly or when you get triggered negatively by something and ask yourself these questions. Why did my mood just change? Why do I feel on edge right now? What happened to make me upset?

Negative emotions often sneak up on us and pull us into a deep dark hole. A few days later, we're still feeling like crap and don't even know why it started in the first place. So next time you find yourself feeling down, don't ignore it. Pay attention, ask questions, and better yet, tell someone. Eventually you'll recover from those kinds of triggers and be able to come back to a place of peace and love within yourself more quickly. This doesn't mean you'll never struggle again, it just means those stressful situations won't take you out for as long as they once did.

The stress of life isn't ever going away. The good news is that you can learn how to deal with it more quickly and find help along the way.

Love always,

Heather

My Prayer for You

God, I pray that You would give my sister the strength and courage to put down the weight she's been carrying and take up Your grace instead. Help her not to be so hard on herself and to know that asking for help and admitting her weaknesses is actually the most powerful thing she can do. Amen.

Soul Selfie

ways to de-stress

Day 1: Bullet Journaling

Use the prompt "Ways to De-Stress" and jot down your ideas in point form. No need for full sentences or perfect handwriting. Pull out some colored pens or pencils and get messy!

Day 2: Live the Letter

Pencil It In (small step)

Ask yourself how you want your life to look and feel in a year. Ask yourself who you would be if you felt completely free from stress and anxiety. Now write that down in a way that inspires you. Next, write a few names of people you think could really help you. They should be people you admire… people you want to be around who you know have wisdom for you.

Put It In Ink (bigger step)

Take the brave step of inviting one of the people from the previous list into your life. You might feel nervous or awkward, but don't worry. Awkward only lasts for a moment, but freedom is forever! The process of opening up and becoming vulnerable isn't easy, so give yourself a pat on the back. Take time to allow yourself to open up and make sure you give yourself props for the progress you're making.

Day 3: Reflection

1. What's one source of stress in your life right now and why?

_____

_____

_____

2. How could you minimize that stress?

_____

_____

_____

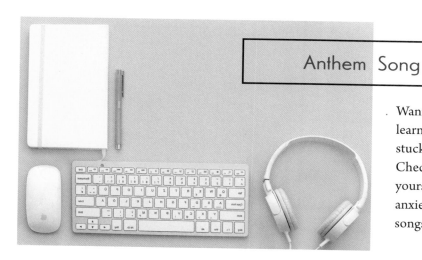

Anthem Song

Want to remember the truth you've learned today? A great way to get truth stuck in your head is through music. Check out this great song to remind yourself to bring your stress, worry, and anxiety to God: "Prince of Peace" by Hillsongs United.

Day 4: Letters from a Big God

Don't just take our word for it—your Creator has a lot to say on this subject. Here are a few verses you can check out to learn more about God's perspective. As you read, ask the Holy Spirit to point out an important verse for you and write it down in your journal, on your mirror, or on a post-it note you can put someplace where you'll see it every day.

Proverbs 27:17

Day 5: Note to Self

Write a short note to yourself or God about the things you've learned from this chapter. What points really stood out to you? What do you want to remember as you go into this next week? How has this chapter changed your perspective about God or yourself?

Dear _____

YOUR

chapter nine

Dean Sister,

When I was sixteen years old, my parents kicked me out of the house. I was a good kid, I loved God, and I was doing well in school. I was involved in extracurricular activities and my youth group. But I was dating a guy my parents didn't approve of. He was older than me and of a different race. I won't get into the details here or seek to defend my parents, but I will say that it was one of the first times I felt the bitter sting of betrayal. The two people I looked up to the most made a decision that made me feel misunderstood and rejected. It felt as if my heart had been ripped out of my chest.

I remember going to youth group that night, and during worship I came undone. I felt myself crumble. I was confused and felt judged and insecure. I was dating someone I thought I loved and was being rejected by my parents for it. Every part of my world felt unsafe.

Once the shock of it passed, the anger came. I was angry with my parents, but mostly I was angry with God. Why would He allow something like this to happen? My heart felt pure and good, yet here I was, cast out and left alone by my own parents. Why would a good God allow this to happen to me?

After a few weeks of staying with random friends and trying to make sense of everything, I eventually made my way back home. I went reluctantly and in a lot of ways felt guilted into returning with little apology or understanding from my parents. But I was sixteen and didn't really have another choice. I still felt misunderstood and angry. The pain was deep and I could feel my heart hardening towards everyone, especially God. Where was He?

Several months went by and I struggled to know how to heal from the experience. Trusting people and God felt scary to me. I was trying to walk through my pain alone, not knowing how to feel, but I was tired and at the end of myself. In a moment of desperation and vulnerability, I opened up to one of my youth leaders. I shared how angry I felt towards God and how I was questioning His goodness. I was surprised to hear her challenge to me.

"Summer, either you believe who God says He is or you don't. There is no middle ground. You need to decide today what you believe or your heart is never going to be the same."

I was shocked by her response. Couldn't she see how much I was hurting? Even though I felt offended, what she said shifted something in me. I was so tired of feeling the loneliness of my pain, not knowing if I could trust God enough to invite Him in to help me heal. I knew I wasn't going to make it if I continued down this road.

If I was ever going to learn how to walk through pain and not be completely shaken about God every time, I would have to decide what I believed about God. I needed to find my anchor. I needed to wrestle through my questions about who He was, and if He was really good. That one conversation encouraged me to challenge God, knowing that if He really was who He said He was, He would show up.

And He did.

I felt God's presence the strongest in the midst of my most desperate, aching, confusing time. My pain pushed me to lean on God and search the Bible to find answers for my aching soul. I'd be lying if I said there weren't times when He felt miles away, silent, and even cruel. I can't explain why we have to go through these things, but when I pressed through without giving up, it gave me a clearer picture of who He is. I learned that He is good, kind, tender, and loves me with a deep love that I'm not sure I'll ever understand. When we are hurting, He wants to hold us close and care for us. He wants to sing over us like a mother sings over her child and put our broken hearts back together.

When I challenged God to show Himself, I found that God actually cared about my pain and that He wasn't the source of it. That's when I found the strength to invite Him and others into my healing process.

Growing up in a Christian home and spending a lot of time in church, I felt like everyone had certain expectations of how I was supposed to carry myself, especially when things were hard. I never had anyone in my life model what it looked like to process pain in a healthy way. I thought I had to be perfect and have everything together, even when I was dying inside. I felt shame for questioning God and struggling with depression.

What I needed was a safe place to wrestle through my questions without feeling judged. I needed to be messy and even fall apart so I could see the pieces of my heart that held pain and shame, and allow God to make me whole again.

I hope my story will encourage you to bring your pain into the light and allow your community and God to help you walk through it into healing. Don't give up, sweet girl. Even though it may hurt now, know that your story isn't over and the best is yet to come.

Love your big sis,

Summer Wright

Thoughts from Heather

I can't imagine what Summer must have felt to be kicked out of her house at sixteen years old. That must have been so hard. But somehow she was able to walk through the pain and come out on the other side, with more strength and courage. I've never gone through anything like that, and I hope you haven't either, but we all experience pain, don't we? And even when we try to run, it seems to chase us down.

Here are some of the things I hope you'll take away from Summer's story.

Decide what you believe about God now, before you walk through hard times. What do you believe about God's nature right now? What you believe about God will directly impact the way you navigate the pain that comes your way. And it will come. I wish I could tell you that you'll walk through your life with only the good, but part of living in this broken world is experiencing pain. If you can build your life on the firm foundation of God's goodness, you can get through anything life throws at you.

Ask hard questions in community. Ask the questions that feel scary to ask, but don't do it alone. Wrestle over these questions in the safety of community and with the guidance of a counsellor or mentor. Let yourself unravel, be messy, and dig into the mess. Just do it with others and with an open invitation to Jesus and the Holy Spirit to guide you. God's not afraid of your questions and He says that when we truly seek Him, we will find Him.

Know that you are not defined by your pain. The most impactful part of your story is who you are becoming through the hard times. Pain is inescapable, but God is good even in the midst of it. As you walk through your pain with Him, know that you are becoming a better version of yourself. Pain experienced with God at your side won't destroy you, but rather shape you into who you were created to be.

So instead of checking out when we feel pain, let's lean into it. Instead of distracting ourselves by scrolling through our Instagram feeds, let's try closing our eyes and taking a deep breath. Instead of running from the mess all around us, let's plop ourselves down right in the middle of it and feel all the hard feelings and face all of our fears.

Guess what you'll find? The pain won't kill you.

The pain you fear so much and work so hard to avoid will come to you as you've never experienced it before. It will come to you as a teacher. A kind and even gentle teacher.

Here's what it will teach you.

1. Experiencing pain opens you up to experiencing love. The best way to deal with the pain of disappointment is radical acceptance. We need to accept that we're going through something hard instead of running from it. When we feel all the hard feelings, we'll find that we have so much more strength and resilience in us than we knew. The pain actually won't crush us! We'll find there is so much more strength and resilience inside us than we knew.

If we can't accept ourselves when we're feeling pain, we can't love ourselves there, or let anyone else love us. But when we accept ourselves in that place of pain, we open the door to a deep and healing love from God, ourselves, and others. If we choose to numb ourselves to pain, we'll also numb ourselves to love and joy. The deeper the pain we feel, the deeper the love.

2. Pain is the gateway to healing. The physical body uses pain as a signal to the brain that an injury has happened, and emotional pain works the same way. If we don't acknowledge our pain, we'll end up walking around with an open, bleeding wound that keeps us from living our best life.

But when we notice the pain and create space for it, we become able to care for the places of brokenness in ourselves and find healing. Without pain, we end up walking through life with a limp instead of dancing through with wholeness. So pay attention to the pain, bring it to God and others, and find healing.

3. Behind the pain is a gift. When we go through something as hard as what Summer did, a gift is often waiting for us on the other side of the experience. If we shut down instead of walking through the pain, we'll miss the gift. But when we allow ourselves to feel the pain instead of rushing past, we'll learn so much about ourselves and about God. We'll find out that we are stronger than we thought, that we're more courageous than we knew. We're able to get through anything with God by our side.

So what is the gift? It's the opportunity to become a better version of ourselves. If we shut down when we feel pain, we'll miss the gift.

Sister, pain doesn't have to be our enemy—though I wouldn't say it's our friend, either. Pain is our teacher. It teaches us how to love ourselves through radical acceptance. It leads us into deeper healing and gives us many beautiful and unexpected gifts. So next time pain visits you, don't run or hide. Stop and sit at its feet and learn everything it has to teach you.

I love you and believe in you so much. You are much stronger than you know.

Love always,

Heather

My Prayer for You

God, You know the pain my sister has gone through and faces even today. Thank You that You are in the middle of our pain and our mess. You don't wait for us to have our act together before coming in close. Help my sister to know that You never do things to cause her pain, but rather You take that pain and turn it around for good. May You heal the places in her heart where she feels broken today. Amen.

Soul Selfie

things that cause me pain

Day 1: Bullet Journaling

Use the prompt "Things that Cause me Pain" and jot down your ideas in point form. No need for full sentences or perfect handwriting. Pull out some colored pens or pencils and get messy!

Day 2: Live the Letter

Pencil It In (small step)

Think of a difficult situation you're going through, or have gone through recently. Write down all the questions you have for God about the situation. Don't leave anything out! Write from your heart and know that He isn't afraid of even your biggest questions. Try to include some "what" questions instead of just "why" questions.

Put It In Ink (bigger step)

Take that list you wrote and share it with someone you trust. Ask them to pray through it with you and together listen for God's response to what you've asked. Remember that when you seek Him with all your heart, you will find Him.

Day 3: Reflection

1. How do you usually respond to painful experiences in your life?

_____

_____

_____

2. How does it affect your faith and beliefs about God when you go through something painful?

_____

_____

_____

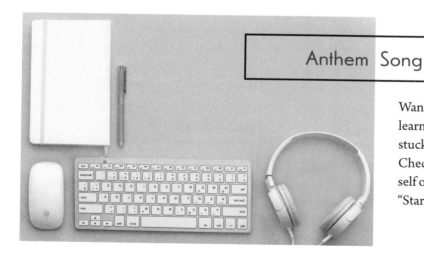

Anthem Song

Want to remember the truth you've learned today? A great way to get truth stuck in your head is through music. Check out this great song to remind yourself of how close God is, even in your pain: "Starlight" by Bethel Music.

Day 4: Letters from a Big God

Don't just take our word for it—your Creator has a lot to say on this subject. Here are a few verses you can check out to learn more about God's perspective. As you read, ask the Holy Spirit to point out an important verse for you and write it down in your journal, on your mirror, or on a post-it note you can put someplace where you'll see it every day.

Psalm 69:28—29, Psalm 73:21—26

Day 5: Note to Self

Write a short note to yourself or God about the things you've learned from this chapter. What points really stood out to you? What do you want to remember as you go into this next week? How has this chapter changed your perspective about God or yourself?

Dear _____

YOUR BEAUTIFUL

reflection

chapter ten

Hey little sis,

I remember the first time I thought negatively about my body. I was on the bus and a boy commented that I had hairy legs and a scar on my knee. I didn't wear anything other than pants for the rest of third grade. Ever since, I've spent too many years picking apart what's wrong with me and what makes me unlike the girls in magazines. I've learned to hate those things about myself.

I've struggled with body image for the better part of my life, always comparing myself to models, the girls on Instagram, or the women who work alongside me. I believe we're taught to compete. We're taught that all other females are our competition and that it's okay to rank ourselves, our bodies, and our successes based on how we compare to them.

But if I've learned anything valuable by this point in my life, it's that I can admire another woman's beauty without questioning my own.

Someday you're going to start to love your body. Trust me when I say it, even though I know it's shocking to hear and hard to believe. After all the years of analyzing and criticizing, eventually you'll get tired of fighting against the one place you can call your home.

Why wait for someday, though? Why not start today?

It's easy to post and talk about body image when my flaws are more hidden, but it's time to just put it all out there and own it. Yes, I have cellulite. Yes, I have rolls. Yes, I have a belly. Yes, I have wrinkles, pimples, and dimples. And yes, I'm still working on loving this body. I need to be reminded, sometimes daily, that I am so worth loving!

Some days are far easier than others, but today I'm challenging you to claim all of it, because maybe as you're reading this you will be reminded that it's okay to not be perfect. It's a big deal when you show up as you are, and it's beautiful to just be *you*.

The old Jenna would have picked this body apart. She would have seen the extra inches spilling over. She would have seen the lack of a thigh gap and googled "leg workouts for thunder thighs." She would've never shared these words for anyone to see! Instead she would have hid under a baggy dress and called it a day.

But I'm not that Jenna anymore. I'm learning to embrace every inch of myself. I'm learning to say out loud, "I'm going to love my body." While saying those words feels like speaking a foreign language, it also feels like being brave.

We all have darkness, imperfections, and mess. It's called being human and it happens when you're alive. See the light in others and treat them as though it's all you can see.

It's easy for me to write to you here and tell you all the reasons why I'm not perfect. But it's hard to tell you what I love about myself. Telling you what's wrong with my size-twelve body is a way to protect myself from you doing it for me.

We have to change the conversation in our heads. These thighs? They love each other so much they can't stop touching. This belly? It held two angel babies for a few months. This body? It's helped me climb some of life's toughest mountains, self-love being among the hardest. And this heart is beating behind this page to remind you that you are enough.

My challenge to you is this: show yourself a little more kindness, a little less judgement. For others, for ourselves, for the world. Be kind. Those two simple words are desperately needed today.

Everyone around you is fighting a battle you know absolutely nothing about, so something tells me you might be fighting your own battle too. Let's be a little slower at flaw-finding and a little quicker to look for the beauty and point it out—in others and in ourselves.

The more humans I meet, the more stories I hear, the more I'm reminded that we are all moving mountains. Some mountains are posted online for the world to see, others are battled behind closed doors. Let kindness lead you today and let that kindness start with *you*.

You're going to do big things, sister. I know it. You just have to look deep within and not focus on the things that you think are imperfect. Those "flaws" are the things that make you captivating, memorable, and beautiful. Trust today that you were made by a Maker who doesn't make any mistakes, and He sure as heck didn't mess up on you!

Love your big sis,

Jenna Kutcher

Thoughts from Heather

I love Jenna's letter so much because in it she shares openly about the struggles many of us face. We *all* have things we dislike about our bodies, yet it's so easy to feel like you're the only one.

It's also easy to compare ourselves to other girls and feel like we don't measure up. One of my favorite lines from Jenna's letter is when she talks about looking at other girls and learning to admire their beauty without questioning our own. Wow! Isn't that amazing?

But how do we get there? How do we get to a place where we appreciate the beauty in others and accept the beauty in ourselves, just the way we are?

1. Remember whose image you were created in. Genesis 1:27 says, *"So God created mankind in his own image, in the image of God he created them; male and female he created them"* (NIV). This passage says that we were created in the image of God, but what does that really mean and how does it apply to loving the girl we see in the mirror?

When I think of being made in God's image, I think of carrying a family resemblance. Every once in a while I run into a friend of my parents' and they'll look at me and say, "Oh, you look like a Wiebe. You have the same nose as your grandpa" or "You have those Derksen eyes, just like your mom."

Except this verse in Genesis explains that instead of just looking like our blood relatives, we actually look like our heavenly Father! When God looks at us, I imagine that He sees a bit of Himself. And even though that resemblance goes way beyond just our looks, it doesn't skip over our physical bodies. God intentionally designed our soul and spirit to live in a body. It wasn't an afterthought or mistake; it was an important part of His design.

So when we curse and hate our bodies, we're insulting their designer as well. Maybe we need to think about that the next time we feel like hating on our thick thighs or curvy booties. We actually carry the DNA of heaven—and that is a reason to love and respect our earthly bodies.

2. Choose thankfulness. There's always something to be grateful for. This is true in your life and it's also true about your body. When you look in the mirror, instead of focusing on the things you don't like, look for the things you're thankful for. Instead of thinking about how big your arms are, be thankful that you have both of them. Instead of wishing for a bigger chest or a smaller waist, be thankful for a healthy heart and the ability to fuel your body with good food.

Thankfulness takes our eyes off the shadows and turns them towards the light. If we look for the bad, we will always find it. But if we look for the good, we will always find that too. What are you looking for when you look at yourself? And what can you be thankful for today?

3. Grow your beauty from the inside out. We girls spend a lot of time and money working on our outer beauty. Whether it's doing our makeup, dying and cutting our hair, shopping for the perfect outfit, or taking it even further with lash extensions, microblading, or sugaring, outer beauty is a big priority for many of us.

And yet our outward appearance is only one piece of the equation. Don't get me wrong, I have no problem with spending some cash on a fun outfit or a great haircut, but we need to consider a few questions. Are we working on our inward beauty as much as our outward appearance? Are we investing in growing our character as much as growing our wardrobe?

A girl who's beautiful on the outside can still come across as very unattractive based on what's on the inside. But I can't say that a girl who's beautiful on the inside *ever* comes across as ugly on the outside. Inner beauty—which is made up of things like kindness, generosity, humor, and integrity—is a way more powerful force than the perfect shade of lipstick or the right name-brand jeans.

My challenge for you is to spend some time working on growing your inner beauty and see how it transforms not only the way people view you, but the way you view yourself.

> *What matters is not your outer appearance—the styling of your hair, the jewelry you wear, the cut of your clothes—but your inner disposition.*
> *Cultivate inner beauty, the gentle, gracious kind that God delights in.*
>
> —1 Peter 3:3–4, MSG

4. Surround yourself with positivity. One of the most powerful ways to grow a positive body image is to hang out with other girls who want to do the same. Maybe that means choosing to spend less time with girls who obsess over their appearance. Make an agreement among your group of friends to only speak positively about yourselves and each other.

This doesn't mean just complimenting one another's outfits or makeup. It means looking for and encouraging the strengths and gifts you see in each other, beyond just looks. Instead of saying how pretty your friend looks, tell her how her smile and presence lights up the room. Instead of commenting on how thin she looks,

celebrate how kind she is. When we focus less on our bodies and more on our hearts, the natural result will be a more positive body image.

Sister, the truth is that you have so much value—and it has nothing to do with the way your body looks. You are valuable because you were created by God and He loves you. You're valuable because you're His daughter, not because you're pretty or not, skinny or not, perfectly proportioned or not. It's time for us to stop buying into the lie that we are only as valuable as the degree to which our bodies match up to society's ideals. It's time for us to put our energy into loving others, creating good things, and changing the world instead of trying to look a certain way.

Love always,

Heather

Side note: If you're really struggling with body image to the point of being tempted by disordered eating, I want to encourage you to reach out for help. Tell your parent, youth pastor, or school counsellor so they can direct you to a professional who can walk with you. There's absolutely no shame in asking for help. In fact, it's one of the most courageous things you can do when you're having a hard time.

My Prayer for You

Jesus, thank You for making my sweet sister fearfully and wonderfully. Help her to align her thoughts with Your thoughts, especially the ones she has about her appearance. Remind her of how perfectly You created her. Remind her that You don't make mistakes and nothing about her is a mistake. Give her the courage to embrace every part of herself and forgive any self-hatred she has partnered with in the past. Amen.

Soul Selfie

what I love about my body

Day 1: Bullet Journaling

Use the prompt "What I Love about my Body" and jot down your ideas in point form. No need for full sentences or perfect handwriting. Pull out some colored pens or pencils and get messy!

Day 2: Live the Letter

Pencil It In (small step)

Next time you look in the mirror when you're getting ready in the morning, pay attention to the things you like about yourself, not just on the outside, but on the inside as well. Look yourself in the eyes and remind yourself out loud how beautiful you are.

Put It In Ink (bigger step)

Choose to do something you never usually do related to your appearance. Maybe that means going a day without makeup, or wearing shorts even though you don't think you have the legs for them. Post a picture on social media that isn't edited and doesn't cut off that part of your body you don't want anyone to see. Run at that fear by doing exactly what it tells you not to do! Notice how you feel after.

Day 3: Reflection

1. What's one negative thought you think regularly about your physical appearance?

_____

_____

_____

2. What do you think God thinks and feels about that part of you?

_____

_____

_____

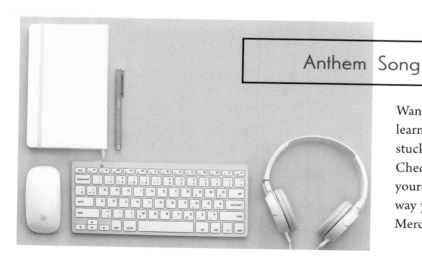

Anthem Song

Want to remember the truth you've learned today? A great way to get truth stuck in your head is through music. Check out this great song to remind yourself of the way God sees you, and the way you can see yourself: "Beautiful" by Mercy Me.

Day 4: Letters from a Big God

Don't just take our word for it—your Creator has a lot to say on this subject. Here are a few verses you can check out to learn more about God's perspective. As you read, ask the Holy Spirit to point out an important verse for you and write it down in your journal, on your mirror, or on a post-it note you can put someplace where you'll see it every day.

Psalm 139

Day 5: Note to Self

Write a short note to yourself or God about the things you've learned from this chapter. What points really stood out to you? What do you want to remember as you go into this next week? How has this chapter changed your perspective about God or yourself?

Dear _____

chapter eleven

Sister,

I'll never forget the summer when I went further with a boy than I ever thought I would. It was the summer between ninth and tenth grade, and I was desperate for attention and love. My parents loved me, I went to church, and I was a happy girl, but I wanted more. I had started to believe that *real* love came from a boy. That real love was physical and it meant giving yourself away to whatever boy you happened to be dating.

Going too far with a boy is something I regret immensely when looking back. It's something I didn't plan to do, and something I had even committed not to let happen. I had signed the pledge cards and gone on a date with my dad where he presented me with a necklace as a reminder of my commitment. Those things couldn't keep me from where that summer led me.

I don't know if you've ever had a moment where you felt sad, embarrassed, and maybe even super guilty for going too far with a boy. If this hasn't happened to you, praise God! If this has happened to a friend of yours, I hope my encouragement can help you to encourage her. And, my sweet friend, if this is your story as well, I want you to lean in close and listen to my words. If we were in person, I would want to hold your hand. I'd look you in the eyes, and you would indeed be the most important person to me at that moment.

You might be struggling with guilt over these mistakes in your life, and I want you to hear me say this: guilt is okay, but it should lead you to repentance. If the guilt you're feeling leads you anywhere besides repentance, then it's not from the Lord. Guilt that leads to shame is not from the Lord. 2 Corinthians reminds us of this when it says, *"Godly sorrow brings repentance that leads to salvation and leaves no regret, but worldly sorrow brings death"* (NIV).

Your guilt should lead you straight to repentance, and let me tell you what happens when you repent: God forgives you. It's what He promises. 1 John 1:9 says, *"If we confess our sins, he is faithful and just and will forgive us our sins and purify us from all unrighteousness"* (NIV). That's the best news ever.

The next thing you need to know is that whatever you've done, however far you've gone, that doesn't define you. You might feel as though it does, and unfortunately someone might imply that you are now "that girl," but let me assure you of something: your mistakes don't define you; the blood of Jesus defines you.

If you are a follower of Jesus, He has declared you right before God. I know that sounds crazy, but I think it's crazy good! None of our failures define us as Christians, or the gospel we believe would be invalid. You see, my friend, you are described as royalty before the Father. You are defined as a daughter of the King. Sister, you are precious to God, and because of Jesus, He sees you as clean. There is great freedom in that, and we can stand before Him clean.

Lastly, you don't have to keep going too far. After that summer, I believed that my mistakes defined me, that God was displeased with me and didn't like me, so I saw no other option other than to be the girl I thought I was. Sweet friend, you don't have to be that girl. God is the God of second chances. If you allow Him, He will guide you into being the woman He desires you to be. Trust me, it's possible. He did that for me and I know He will do it for you.

You are cared for and deeply loved. Jesus is way bigger than any mistake you could ever make, and you are not used goods. Your past doesn't define you. Don't let it. Hold your head up high, continue to chase after God, love His word, and you'll be just fine.

Love your big sister,

Jamie Ivey

Thoughts from Heather

I don't know about you, but I can relate to Jamie's story. I was also in a relationship when I was seventeen and went further physically than I ever planned on going. Even though I didn't actually have sex with the guy, I compromised my boundaries and felt so much guilt and shame about it. I tried to deal with that guilt by staying in a relationship I knew wasn't healthy. I thought, at least if we get married one day it will make all of these wrong things right. It was such a messed-up way of thinking, but it's all I knew. I didn't realize that I wasn't damaged goods. I didn't realize that God would forgive me and give me a clean slate. A fresh start. I didn't realize who I truly was as a daughter of God.

I love how Jamie reminds us that guilt which doesn't lead to repentance isn't from God. The word repentance actually means to do a 180-degree turn, to turn our backs on our old way and move towards God's way. What we often don't realize is that we have to do a 180-degree turn in the way we think, not just the way we act. If we don't believe we're forgiven, we won't live as though we're forgiven. If we try to will our way into behaving better, we'll fail over and over again. We'll just keep being "that girl"—that girl who goes too far with boys, or that girl who doesn't keep her word, or that girl who's always talking about her friends behind their backs. The only way to stop being that girl is to stop thinking you are that girl.

True change comes when we change the way we think.

Romans 12:2 says, *"Do not conform to the pattern of this world, but be transformed by the renewing of your mind"* (NIV). But what does it mean to renew our minds? I like to use this acronym to help explain what it means: RENEW.

Recognize the lie you've been believing. Pay attention to the thoughts you're having and notice what lies are creeping in.

Evaluate the lies against the truth of God's Word. If your thought doesn't line up with truth, replace the lie with the truth.

Notice your triggers. What things set you off to start thinking in those negative patterns? What words or actions from others seem to trigger those lies? Paying attention to your triggers will help you snap out of the negative spiral more quickly.

End that story. Every time that old story starts playing in your head, press stop. Not pause, rewind, and repeat—just *full stop*. Try to do it as quickly as you can. It will be hard at first, but I promise it will get easier and easier with time and practice.

Walk the other way. Whatever a 180-degree turn looks like in the moment, do it. Think new thoughts. Start new habits. You might even need to find new people to hang out with. If you truly want a renewed mind and transformed life, walking the other way is a key step in getting there.

As your mind is renewed by the truth of God's Word, it will actually get easier to live a different way. It won't feel like you're trying and failing over and over again. Eventually you won't even *want* to do the things that were so tempting before. This is when you know you're truly being transformed.

Sister, if you're in a situation like Jamie was and you've gone too far with a guy, you need to know that you're not damaged goods. You are not too far gone. Your chances at future happiness are not ruined. But you do have a very important choice to make. Are you going to continue thinking and living the way you have been or are you going to repent?

Maybe you feel stuck and don't know how or where to start, so I'm going to give you a few steps to help get you unstuck.

1. Start to renew your mind using the guidelines above. Remember, this isn't just about the way you act, but also the way you think.

2. Have an honest conversation with your boyfriend about boundaries. I'm not going to go into great detail about what your boundaries should be, but if you haven't already, have this conversation with the person you're dating. Decide beforehand what's okay and what's not okay, not in the heat of the moment. If you don't feel like you can be this honest with your boyfriend, he might not be a great person for you to be dating.

3. Talk to a trusted friend or mentor about what you're going through. You don't have to walk through this alone. One of the best ways to break the power of shame and guilt is to tell someone about your struggle. It would also be helpful to get input from your mentor about some appropriate boundaries to set in your relationship moving forward.

4. Take a break. It might be helpful to take a week or two to have some space from your boyfriend. I know, I know… for some of you, this sounds like absolute torture. But it's not breaking up. It's just taking a step back

to re-evaluate, gain some perspective, and make a plan for moving forward in a way you'll feel good about. Just think about it, okay?

I know I've said this many times before, but I want to remind you how incredibly valuable you are. No matter what mistakes you've made or how far you've gone, you are never too far away for God to reach you. He is insanely in love with you. Even at your lowest, He is holding you up. If you hear nothing else, please hear this: *"Surely the arm of the Lord is not too short to save, nor his ear too dull to hear"* (Isaiah 59:1, NIV).

He is listening. He is reaching. Will you reach back?

Love always,

Heather

My Prayer for You

God, I thank You that in You my sister is never stuck. In You, all things are working together for her good. You are actively moving on her behalf. Your Spirit is such a powerful force! I pray that she would experience the power of Your Spirit moving in her life this week. Give her the self-discipline to follow through with the steps You've revealed to her. Let her see the transformation that comes through walking with You. Amen.

change feels like...

Day 1: Bullet Journaling

Use the prompt "Change feels like…" and jot down your ideas in point form. No need for full sentences or perfect handwriting. Pull out some colored pens or pencils and get messy!

Day 2: Live the Letter

Pencil It In (small step)

Look back at the steps for how to get un-stuck and choose one that you can do this week. Which one are you going to choose and why? Write your answer here and the date by which you plan to complete it.

Put It In Ink (bigger step)

Share the one step you're going to take with a friend or mentor and challenge them to take one as well. Pray for each other and hold one another accountable to take that step by the time you said you would.

Day 3: Reflection

1. How do you usually respond when you make a mistake? What about when someone in your life messes up?

_____

_____

_____

2. Do you agree that a transformed mind equals a transformed life? Why or why not?

_____

_____

_____

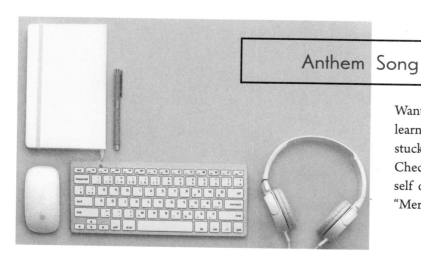

Anthem Song

Want to remember the truth you've learned today? A great way to get truth stuck in your head is through music. Check out this great song to remind yourself of how God responds to our mess: "Mercy" by Amanda Cook.

Day 4: Letters from a Big God

Don't just take our word for it—your Creator has a lot to say on this subject. Here are a few verses you can check out to learn more about God's perspective. As you read, ask the Holy Spirit to point out an important verse for you and write it down in your journal, on your mirror, or on a post-it note you can put someplace where you'll see it every day.

Romans 8:32, Philippians 4: 8—9

Day 5: Note to Self

Write a short note to yourself or God about the things you've learned from this chapter. What points really stood out to you? What do you want to remember as you go into this next week? How has this chapter changed your perspective about God or yourself?

Dear _____

YOUR LIGHT IS

brighten

chapter twelve

Sweet girl,

There's something I want to remind you of today, a truth which may seem small and simple yet has the potential to transform your life.

I want to remind you of the light inside you, the light that came and made a home in your heart the moment you realized you needed God. When you said yes to Jesus, invited Him in, and allowed Him to take away the dirt and grime of your life, He made you brand new. It was like a lightbulb was switched on inside you, and the light filled you from the top of your head to the tip of your toes. You became a carrier of His truth, His hope, and His joy.

Back in England where I'm from, I grew up singing a little song which you may have sung too: "This little light of mine, I'm gonna let it shine." It's such a sweet song, but it isn't fully in line with the truth of God's Word.

What do you think of as you sing these words? As a young girl, I always imagined that inside me I had a small, delicate flicker of God's light, a feeble flame deep down in my soul. I saw myself bravely yet weakly shining in the vast darkness. The light was something I needed to protect from being blown out. I didn't realize it at the time, but believing that the light of God inside me was small and insignificant was an untruth that held me back and kept me living in fear. I was afraid that as I went out into a dark world my little light might be snuffed out. I feared that the darkness out there was more powerful than my little flame.

Dear one, I want to tell you today that the light you have inside you isn't small. In fact, it's so strong that it fills the whole of you. As 1 Thessalonians 5:5 says, *"You are all children of the light and children of the day. We do not belong to the night or to the darkness"* (NIV). You are not some pale reflection of the light, as the moon reflects the sun. You *are* light—the whole of you. A great glowing furnace of light, fierce and strong, shines out of you.

And this light isn't actually yours. It's God's light. He is the one who put it inside you and He invites you to walk hand in hand with Him. As you do, He will naturally shine through each part of you. You need not scheme and plan and fret about how people will see the light inside you. The more you're aware of His light inside you, the brighter it will shine.

Have you ever noticed that light always wins? Darkness can look so scary, yet it's simply a place where there isn't any light. When light comes, darkness cannot stay. When light comes, darkness has to go. Know, dear one, that when you walk into a room, everything changes.

That light you have inside you is always there, yet sometimes in the busyness of life we get distant from God and forget who we are and who is inside us. I often pause in my day to ask the Father, "Would you help me to know what it means to have your light inside me?" In those moments, I become aware of the fire inside me again.

Understanding the power and presence within you changes everything. Some of the most precious moments in my life have been those when others have commented, "Hannah, you're different from other people. When I'm with you, I feel peaceful, I feel safe, I feel loved, and I can be myself." It's not really because of anything I've said or done. It's mostly because I'm a carrier of the light of His love.

Colossians 1:27 refers to *"Christ in [me], the hope of glory"* (NIV). I want to be someone who carries the glory and hope of God. Imagine that you became so aware of the power of God in you that you could touch someone and they could feel the presence of God like never before. They might even be healed because of His glory inside you. That would be amazing! That's my dream for me and for you.

I wish I had known this truth more when I was younger. I think it would have made me so much more confident.

The enemy has one battle plan, and it is to make you feel weak, helpless, and insecure, to blind you from the power within you. If he can keep you believing those things, you won't walk in the power of the light.

As you read this letter today, I trust that you will begin a new season of being aware of the glory and power of God that you carry to the world. Become more aware of His presence inside you. Pray "God, show me what it means to carry Your light" so that you might begin to see the effect of this truth in your life.

Love your big sis,

Hannah Giddens

Thoughts from Heather

So much of what Hannah shared reminds me of these two words: *free* and *powerful*. Sister, you aren't a victim of circumstance. You aren't easily crushed by the challenges of life. You are full of strength and grit—not because you try hard and perform well, but because of God's light inside you. You are free and you are powerful.

Everything changes when we view ourselves as powerful instead of victims. I know this because at the beginning of eighth grade, I saw myself as a victim. I didn't have a lot of friends, didn't make the volleyball team, and definitely wasn't getting any attention from the cute boys in my class. To top it all off, I was having a big ole pity party about it.

If they would just be nice to me, if only that coach would have given me a chance, if that cute guy would just take the time to get to know me, then I would be happy, I thought to myself. *Then my life would be good.*

Instead of seeing myself as free and powerful to make choices that would shape my life, I was waiting for my circumstances to change. Instead of recognizing the light that was inside me, I was hiding in the dark, waiting for someone else to come shine their light and brighten my day.

Even though I didn't have many close friends, I did have a few amazing mentors. One of them suggested I read Sean Covey's *7 Habits of Highly Effective Teens*. At first I thought it sounded pretty lame, but I was quickly drawn in.

The first habit described in the book is about being proactive.

Being proactive is more than taking initiative. It is recognizing that we are responsible for our own choices and have the freedom to choose based on principles and values rather than on moods or condition. Proactive people are agents of change and choose not to be victims, to be reactive, or to blame others.[5]

---

5   Stephen Covey, "Being proactive is more…" *AZ Quotes.* Date of access: November 8, 2011 (https://www.azquotes.com/quote/1467283).

Reading these words was a kick in the butt for me because I had been making a lot of choices based on my mood and circumstance, which were both pretty negative. Instead of choosing to shine my light, I was believing that the darkness around me would swallow me up.

But as I embraced the truth that I was powerful to make choices that would point me in the direction I wanted it to go, I started to see change. I felt happier even though I still didn't have a ton of friends and life wasn't perfect. Instead of trying to control those things, I chose to accept responsibility for my attitude and reactions. I decided to shine my light, whether I felt like it or not.

And as it turns out, my light wasn't so little after all.

His Presence, Your Light

So what is that light inside us, that thing that makes us free and powerful instead of victims of circumstances? It's the presence of God—the Holy Spirit. When you say yes to following Jesus, you are given the gift of His Spirit.

So if it's true that we have the Holy Spirit inside us, making us free and powerful, why don't we always live in free and powerful ways? Why do we get stuck in unhealthy patterns of thinking? Why do we so often default to being victims of circumstance? It's because we get disconnected from our power source. It's like a lamp sitting right beside an electrical outlet, but the cord isn't plugged in. How do we stay plugged into the power source of His presence?

Worship

We were created to worship God, designed to remain in close connection to Him at all times. We are most fully ourselves when we're focused on Him instead of on ourselves or what's going on around us.

Worship isn't just about singing songs on a Sunday morning. Worship happens every time we turn our attention and affection towards Him—as we study, work, play, or even rest. Yes, even you lounging around the house can be an act of worship when you're mindful of the fact that God is right there with you.

Worship is liking plugging that lamp into the outlet. It's remembering that He is the source. It can be as simple as a whispered prayer: "Hi God. I know you're here. Thanks for being close." It can be as extravagant as singing at the top of your lungs and dancing your heart out. And it can be as unassuming as washing the dishes with a heart to please God. When we worship, we draw near to Him and He draws near to us.

Sometimes when I start to feel a victim mindset coming on, or when I'm discouraged by the way my day is unfolding, I worship by taking a few deep breaths. As I breathe in, I remember that His love holds all the cells of my being together, and His love is complete. He doesn't just love the part of me that's getting it right. He loves all of me. He loves the mess and the struggle and the failure I can be. When I take these deep breaths and reconnect with His love, I'm reconnecting with the power source of His Spirit in me.

Declarations

Using our words to speak the truth out loud is a powerful way to stay connected to the light inside us. We're so quick to use our words to speak negatively or give voice to our worries and complaints, but how often do we remember to use our words to speak the truth, even when we aren't feeling it?

One of the ways we can do this is by talking to our spirits. I know, it sounds a little weird, but stick with me. Human beings are made up of a body, soul, and spirit. But how often do we actually let our spirits lead us? Usually we make decisions based on our emotions or our thoughts, both of which come from our soul (the mind, will, and emotions). But the Holy Spirit lives in our spirit, so that's really our greatest place of strength. The trick is learning how to activate your spirit to lead rather than letting your thoughts and emotions run the show.

One way to do this is to actually speak out loud to your spirit and tell it to take the lead. The next time you feel that dark cloud of depression come over you, try saying, "Depression and darkness, step aside. Joy, I give you permission to lead me." You may actually feel the joy come up in you—or you may feel nothing, but the truth is that you will have empowered the Spirit of joy to lead your life and decisions in that moment. You will have plugged the cord into the power source and turned the light back on.

When we live with the belief that we always have access to God's presence, even if our emotions tell us something else, we know that the truth is even more powerful than those feelings.

Love always,

Heather

My Prayer for You

Father, I thank You for the incredible light You've placed inside my sister. I pray that she would realize how powerful that light is. It cannot be snuffed out. It can be covered by fear or shame or guilt, but it can't be turned off. May she learn how to let that light shine brightly and without fear of what others will think. Amen.

ways I shine my light

Day 1: Bullet Journaling

Use the prompt "Ways I Shine my Light" and jot down your ideas in point form. No need for full sentences or perfect handwriting. Pull out some colored pens or pencils and get messy!

Day 2: Live the Letter

Pencil It In (small step)

Grab some post-it notes and write down a few short verses about being a light. Go around your house, or just your room, and put the sticky notes above your light switches and on your lamps. Every time you turn the lights on or off, remind yourself of the light inside you that can never be turned off.

Put It In Ink (bigger step)

Write out a list of three ways you can be a light this week, in the following categories: in your family, in your school, and in your community. Now do it! Try shining your light, then watch and see what happens and how you feel.

Day 3: Reflection

1. What's one thing that holds you back from shining your light?

_____

_____

_____

2. What does total freedom look like to you? What would you do differently if you knew that every word you spoke and decision you made was either bringing more light or more darkness into the world? _____

_____

_____

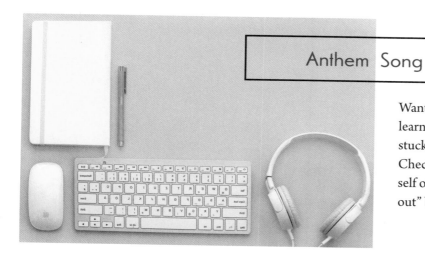

Anthem Song

Want to remember the truth you've learned today? A great way to get truth stuck in your head is through music. Check out this great song to remind yourself of the brightness of your light: "Blackout" by Steffany Gretzinger.

Day 4: Letters from a Big God

Don't just take our word for it—your Creator has a lot to say on this subject. Here are a few verses you can check out to learn more about God's perspective. As you read, ask the Holy Spirit to point out an important verse for you and write it down in your journal, on your mirror, or on a post-it note you can put someplace where you'll see it every day.

Galatians 5:1, Matthew 5:14—16

Day 5: Note to Self

Write a short note to yourself or God about the things you've learned from this chapter. What points really stood out to you? What do you want to remember as you go into this next week? How has this chapter changed your perspective about God or yourself?

Dear _____

YOU ARE NOT

your past

_____

chapter thirteen

My sweet sister,

Growing up, I believed I had the perfect family. We had a beautiful house in a great neighborhood. I never wanted for anything, and I was happy and loved.

It wasn't until my parents decided to split up that my safe little world shattered into a million pieces. I felt blindsided, confused, angry, and deeply hurt. My thirteen-year old heart was broken when I faced the reality that my dad wanted to leave us. Leave *me*. What had I done wrong? What was so unlovable about me that he had changed his mind about me? What could I do to win him back?

I believe that something profound happens deep in your spirit when the one place in your world that is meant to be safe—your home, your very family—breaks in two. Just as an earthquake cracks the earth apart, you sense of self and security will be fractured, and the aftershocks will be felt for years to come.

I spent most of my teenage years reeling from my parents' decision and it deeply impacted how I viewed myself, others, and even God. Because I felt that my dad had rejected me, I constantly worried about being left behind. On the outside, I appeared confident, but on the inside I agonized over the prospect of friends abandoning me, leaders and teachers disapproving of me, and family members being taken away. I experienced a lot of anxiety.

In high school, I watched my friends and classmates with their boyfriends and girlfriends, and I couldn't fathom that someone could actually love me like that. I wanted so badly to date, to experience all the fun of a relationship, but I was scared to open my heart.

Although I stayed close to Jesus during those tumultuous years, I saw Him through a distorted lens, blurred by the pain I was experiencing. I felt that He loved me, but He could easily change His mind if I wasn't perfectly lovable. So I worked very hard to be a good girl, to never disappoint, to do all the right things, to be worthy of His love.

A pivotal moment arrived when I was nineteen years old. While talking with my best friend about the latest drama in my family, and she dropped an unexpected and much-needed truth bomb: "You know, Alisha, eventually you're going to have to stop blaming your parents for what happened to you and realize you have your own beautiful life to live."

I was a bit taken aback and my defenses went up. It was *their* fault. *They* had caused all this pain!

But over time I realized how right she was. Of course my parents' choices had hurt me, and even altered the direction of my life, but they didn't define who I was. I could choose to continue to feel victimized by their actions or I could forgive my parents and move forward in freedom. I slowly began to accept the possibility of holding the pain of my past *and* celebrating the potential of my future. This revelation led to healing.

In His grace, the Lord never abandoned me. He provided for me, proved His unconditional love, and gave me hope. I got to know some older couples who became role models of healthy relationships. God also gifted me with a community that pushed me to grow, heal, and lean into the woman I was born to become. It was often a struggle, but I can say without hesitation that it was worth it to experience the depth of the Father's love.

Little sis, you may see yourself in my story. If you do, I'm so sorry that you've had to endure the pain of living in a broken family. You are not alone. While your experience right now is difficult and painful, maybe even unbearable at times, you need to know that it's not the end of your story. In the midst of chaos, your Heavenly Father is holding you close and comforting your broken heart. You can trust Him with your pain. You can lean into Him and rest, crawl into His lap, and sink into His soft, fierce love for you. As you do, remember the truth He spoke to me as a broken young girl fighting for wholeness.

You are worthy. You are the Father's beloved daughter. You are completely and wholly His masterpiece. God's intention for you has always been to give you purpose and value. Because He made you in His image, you are no longer bound by darkness, pain, or suffering—you are free to love and be loved.

You cannot earn the Father's love. No amount of doing or striving will change the depth of His love for you. He is the endless fountain of love, forever overflowing with goodness and grace. This love is never dependent on your good behavior. You will miss the mark sometimes, but God's heart will never skip a beat.

Your parents' decisions don't define you. You aren't doomed to failed relationships and your family's shortcomings are not your shortcomings. Yes, your family's brokenness is a part of you, but don't forget that it's simply one chapter in your life's book. God will always work to redeem what is broken and breathe new life into dead bones.

Sweet sister, when you pursue the heart of God and lean into His unrelenting love, I promise you will experience a fullness and confidence you never thought possible. The Father will fill your heart, mind, and spirit with a deep, abiding love to carry you through the mess. He will give you hope and the promise of a beautiful future because He loves you with the perfect love of a Parent who never fails.

Your sister,

Alisha McKay

Thoughts from Heather

Alisha's story shows us how powerful it is to take ownership of our lives. When things go wrong and we can't control our circumstances, we *can* control our response to those circumstances. This doesn't mean we shut down our emotions and pretend it isn't hard. It just means we don't let those emotions make our decisions for us. Emotions are a great "check engine" light to remind us to pay attention to what's going on in our lives, and even warn us about potential danger.

A turning point for Alisha came when her friend challenged her to stop blaming her parents for the past and start focusing on the future she was creating with God. Even though it was hard for her to hear this truth, everything changed when she did. This is what happens when we start showing up in our own lives. We get unstuck. We stop looking back at our past and feeling sorry for ourselves for how hard we had it. We start looking ahead to our future, dreaming about what's possible and partnering with the Holy Spirit to make it happen.

In drivers ed, you learn not to spend too much time looking in the rear-view mirror, because you can't control what's going on behind you. Even if you see it coming, you can't stop someone from rear-ending you. What you can do is pay attention to what's in front of you.

The same is true in life. If you're constantly focused on the past and how hard it's been, or how unfair it was, you aren't living in a powerful way. In fact, you're much like a driver who only looks in the rear-view mirror. Not only will this keep you stuck in the past, it could damage what would otherwise be a beautiful future. You have so much more power over how you'll walk into your future than how you've lived through your past.

When we're unable to forgive those who've hurt us, or let go of injustices done to us, we bring that hurt into our current and future relationships. We put up walls and distance ourselves—not because a new friend has shown herself to be untrustworthy, but because that person from our past was. Do you see how that past pain can rob you of future joy?

Here are some important truths I want remind you about, sweet sister.

- Just because your parents' marriage didn't work out doesn't mean you won't have a beautiful marriage one day.
- Just because your mom is harsh with you doesn't mean you won't be an incredible mom.
- Just because all you knew as a child was brokenness and fear doesn't mean your children are destined for the same experience.

It's time to let go of the past. It's time to dive headfirst into your bright and beautiful future! It's time to take a huge leap of faith and trust that God is actually who He says He is—a good Father who is working everything together for your good. I can tell you from experience that when you trust Him He takes every painful thing from your past and turns it around for your good. In the areas where you felt most robbed, He brings restoration. Where you were wounded, He brings healing. Where you were disappointed, He brings hope.

God isn't going to leave you where you are, but He's also not going to force you to move forward. He is extending His hand in invitation to you today, inviting you into a bright future. Not an easy one, but one filled with hope and possibility because of His power at work in your life.

Philippians 1:6 says, *"[B]eing confident of this, that he who began a good work in you will carry it on to completion until the day of Christ Jesus"* (NIV).

If it's not good yet, it's because He's not finished yet!

Love always,

Heather

My Prayer for You

God, thank You for being with my little sister through all the hard things she has walked through. Heal her from past hurts and protect her from slipping into a victim mindset. Remind her of how much You love her and what a bright future she has in front of her. Thank You for Your love and faithfulness and that all of Your promises are yes and amen!

Soul Selfie

favorite childhood memories

Day 1: Bullet Journaling

Use the prompt "Favorite Childhood Memories" and jot down your ideas in point form. No need for full sentences or perfect handwriting. Pull out some colored pens or pencils and get messy!

Day 2: Live the Letter

Pencil It In (small step)

Write a letter of forgiveness to someone from your past who hurt you. Be honest about how their actions affected you and made you feel. Tell them why you're forgiving them and how you hope to see the relationship look in the future. You don't have to send the letter, but if you want to then go ahead.

Put It In Ink (bigger step)

Take some time to imagine what you want your future to look like. Write it out, paint a picture, make a collage, start a Pinterest folder—whatever works for you. Now share what you've created with a close friend or mentor. Pray together and ask God to do something great in your life. Ask Him to help you stop looking back and instead fix your eyes on the bright future ahead.

Day 3: Reflection

1. What's one thing that was really hard about your childhood?

_____

_____

_____

2. What's one thing you are super grateful for about the way you grew up?

_____

_____

_____

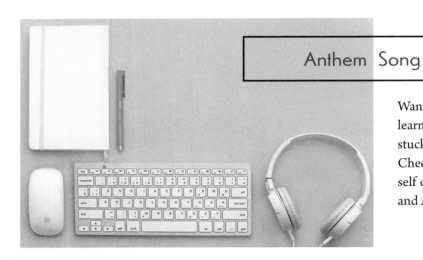

Anthem Song

Want to remember the truth you've learned today? A great way to get truth stuck in your head is through music. Check out this great song to remind yourself of your bright future with Jesus: "Yes and Amen" by Housefires.

Day 4: Letters from a Big God

Don't just take our word for it—your Creator has a lot to say on this subject. Here are a few verses you can check out to learn more about God's perspective. As you read, ask the Holy Spirit to point out an important verse for you and write it down in your journal, on your mirror, or on a post-it note you can put someplace where you'll see it every day.

Jeremiah 29:11, Philippians 3:13—14

Day 5: Note to Self

Write a short note to yourself or God about the things you've learned from this chapter. What points really stood out to you? What do you want to remember as you go into this next week? How has this chapter changed your perspective about God or yourself?

Dear _____

YOUR SECRET WORLD-CHANGING

weapon

chapter fourteen

Dear Little Sister,

On my sixteenth birthday, I stepped out the front door of our house to see a gleaming, yellow 1968 Ford Mustang. Tied around its sleek coupe doors and its jutted-out nose was a ridiculously giant red bow. My dad had been secretly restoring this car for me for months. Even though I didn't know what a Mustang was and this wanting-to-fit-in teenager wasn't ecstatic about the color, I knew this car represented my dad's deep love for me.

All told, I got into six accidents that year. Yes, six! My beautiful shiny car took a beating. My dad was patient with the first five fender-benders, but somehow I just knew the sixth one was going to send him over the edge. Mom called Dad at work to break the news of my latest driving fiasco.

As I waited in my room for my dad to get home, a million emotions rolled through me. I thought about the hours upon hours he had spent working on that car. I thought about how much love and sweat he'd poured into this precious gift. He had considered me in every detail. I felt terrible that I had been so reckless. I felt as though I had failed him.

After what seemed like an eternity, his cowboy boots scaled the steps and I heard him take the final steps toward my door. I prepared to meet my end, bracing myself as I turned to face him. I expected to see anger, frustration, or disappointment, but instead I saw his kind eyes looking at me over a giant bouquet. He had shown up not to condemn me, but to show me compassion. Not with judgment, but with flowers.

That moment with my dad has marked me for life. I deserved to be yelled at. I would have understood losing my driving privileges for a while. Instead he gave me compassion. I had been excited by the gift of the car, but I was changed by this gift of compassion.

I didn't know it at the time, but the lesson I learned from my dad this day became a foundational principle of my life. We live in a world in which compassion is rare. Compassion means that you feel something so deeply for another person that you are compelled to make every sacrifice to help alleviate or bring change to their painful experience. Compassion holds the power to transform a situation.

The gospel of John tells the story of a group of religious scholars who paraded through the streets a woman who had been caught in the midst of adultery. They shoved her in front of Jesus while blaring her charges out to the crowds. Because the punishment for getting caught in the act of adultery was stoning, she was to be forced to kneel while they legally threw stones at her until she died.

Jesus looked at her accusers, their angry fists gripped around the jagged edges of the stones, and then turned to look at the woman. The fear and shame in her eyes met the mercy in His. Her accusers demanded that she receive punishment to the full extent of the law, but He bent down and began writing in the sand.

They continued yelling at him until He finally stood up and said, *"Let any of you who is without sin among you be the first to throw a stone at her"* (John 8:7, NIV) As He bent down to his writing again, one by one she heard the stones that had been meant for her fall to the ground.

I may not be able to stop others from throwing their proverbial stones, but I can be the change I wish to see in the world, as Gandhi said. I don't want to be the person bringing shame any more than I want to be the person being shamed. I want to be like Jesus. I want to be like my dad. I want to be the person who enters the hostile and toxic spaces of the world and gives compassion. Compassion is the only thing that can transform and change the dynamic of a world that is bent on throwing condemnation.

Just as Jesus stepped in with compassion for this woman, He has stepped in for you too. He has taken on all of your failings, your shame, and your brokenness and given you tender mercies, compassion, and unrivalled love. What my dad showed me that day was mercy. This single act of kindness I didn't deserve disrupted the shame storyline I had been writing for myself. The compassion I received that day changed me, because compassion possesses the power to transform, to shift, to cause us to disregard the stories that belittle us and instead come face to face with the worth that has been ours all along.

Sweet sister, be the person who steps in with compassion and mercy to a world that is crushed under the burden of condemnation. When the world expects you to show up with stones, be the one who shows up with a giant bouquet of compassion.

With love,

Jessica Honneger

Thoughts from Heather

Reading Jessica's letter may have brought up all kinds of thoughts and feelings for you. Some of you might relate to the way Jessica's dad responded to her sixth car accident with grace and compassion. Some of you might just relate to the six accidents! (Any other distracted drivers out there?) And some of you might be wishing you had a dad like that. The truth is, so many of us haven't experienced that kind of compassion from our earthly fathers. But the good news is that we all have access to a Dad like this, our Father in heaven.

Praise be to the God and Father of our Lord Jesus Christ, the Father of compassion and the God of all comfort, who comforts us in all our troubles, so that we can comfort those in any trouble with the comfort we ourselves receive from God.

—2 Corinthians 1:3–4, NIV

These verses are full of so much powerful truth that emphasizes everything Jessica shared in her story. Our God is the Father of compassion. He is the God of *all* comfort. His response isn't to have compassion sometimes and then when we mess up one too many times explode with the anger that's been building up all along. No, that's not what our Dad is like. He comforts us in *all our troubles*, even the troubles we cause for ourselves. He doesn't just comfort us when it's someone else's fault. He comforts us even when it's one hundred percent our fault. His compassion isn't based on our behavior. It's grounded in His love.

When we open ourselves up to receive His compassion and comfort in the most painful and messed up parts of our lives, it does something incredible. It moves us to share this same compassion and comfort with others. When we taste a love this sweet, we want to share it with everyone we know!

This passage from 2 Corinthians says that we are comforted with a purpose. That purpose isn't just feeling better so can go on our merry way. The purpose is passing that comfort on to those who are hurting around us.

We haven't been given all we've been given just for our own benefit. We've been given it so we can give it away to others. We are comforted not so we can be comfortable, but so we can comfort others.

What does this mean for you?

Well, sister, it means that the next time you're hurting, you can choose not to stay stuck in that hard place alone. You can reach out to your heavenly Father and find compassion and comfort in His presence. You can pour out your whole heart to Him.

For me, this looks like going someplace where I can be alone and screaming at the top of my lungs. It looks like crying my guts out, not holding anything back.

He can handle our pain. He can take our anger. He can hold our sadness. And His response to all of it is compassion and comfort. Every. Single. Time.

And it means the next time you see someone hurting, you don't stand by and watch. You get up off your butt and walk over to that person, place your hand on their shoulder, look into their eyes, and share the comfort you've received. It means that we no longer sit back and feel bad for people but do nothing to help them. It means we act. We move. We show compassion even if it costs us our own comfort.

Sister, if you and I are moved by compassion to action, our world will change. If we open our hearts to be comforted first, and then give that comfort away freely and generously, the darkness will be pushed back. If we take that bouquet of compassion we've been given and start handing those flowers out to everyone around us, the joy and love *will* spread.

If the idea of reaching out to share comfort with someone makes you incredibly uncomfortable, you aren't alone. I've been following Jesus for nearly my whole life and I still find it challenging, and sometimes awkward, to show compassion to the people around me. Not so much with my friends and family, but with people outside of my close circle.

Instead of feeling bad about this and using it as another excuse to do nothing, consider this: maybe the reason you have trouble reaching out to someone who's hurting in a certain way is because that's an area where you are still experiencing pain yourself. For example, if seeing insecurity in others makes you feel like you want nothing to do with them, it could be that you struggle with that same insecurity. Instead of following the gut reaction to run away, maybe you need to look inward and ask yourself, "Why do I struggle to show compassion to that person? Is there anything in me that still needs healing in that area?"

When we are triggered by other people's struggles, it's often because we share that same struggle. Don't ignore those triggers. Pay attention to them and ask yourself and God questions about them.

Sister, you are a world-changer. It's already inside of you. Now it's time to let it out!

Love always,

Heather

My Prayer for You

Thank You that You are a God of comfort and compassion. I pray that You'd comfort my sister today. Flow into all of the places in her life where there is pain and bring healing. Give her a heart of compassion for herself and for others. Use her to release Your love into this hurting world. Thank You for who she is and all that she carries. Help her to see herself the way You do. Amen.

Soul Selfie

compassion looks like...

Day 1: Bullet Journaling

Use the prompt "Compassion looks like…" and jot down your ideas in point form. No need for full sentences or perfect handwriting. Pull out some colored pens or pencils and get messy!

Day 2: Live the Letter

Pencil It In (small step)

Imagine someone in pain. Imagine what they look like, sound like, and feel like. Imagine yourself approaching them to show comfort and compassion. What does that look like, sound like, feel like? Imagine what you say and do to help them. Picture how they respond to the love you're showing them. What changes in the way they look, sound, feel? How does it make you feel to see that transformation?

Put It In Ink (bigger step)

Ask the Holy Spirit to bring someone to your mind who's in need of comfort. Write down three different ways you can reach out to that person this week. Now choose one of those ideas and do it this week. If this brings up feelings of fear or anxiety, talk to God about that.

Day 3: Reflection

1. Describe a time when you were comforted by someone. What did that look like? Feel like?

_____

_____

_____

2. What part of that experience can you repeat and share with someone you know who is hurting?

_____

_____

_____

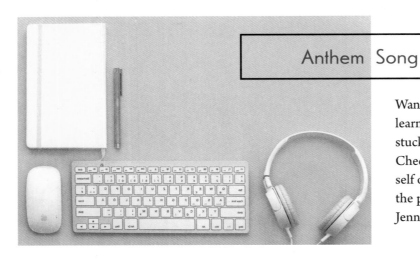

Anthem Song

Want to remember the truth you've learned today? A great way to get truth stuck in your head is through music. Check out this great song to remind yourself of the way God has called you to love the people around you: "For the One" by Jenn Johnson.

Day 4: Letters from a Big God

Don't just take our word for it—your Creator has a lot to say on this subject. Here are a few verses you can check out to learn more about God's perspective. As you read, ask the Holy Spirit to point out an important verse for you and write it down in your journal, on your mirror, or on a post-it note you can put someplace where you'll see it every day.

Psalm 103:8—13, Philippians 2:1—4

Day 5: Note to Self

Write a short note to yourself or God about the things you've learned from this chapter. What points really stood out to you? What do you want to remember as you go into this next week? How has this chapter changed your perspective about God or yourself?

Dear _____

Sister,

You made it to the end! Thank you so much for taking the time to read these letters. I hope and pray that you've been able to find pieces of your story along the way and know now more than ever that you are not alone. You are surrounded by a tribe of big sisters who love and believe in you so much.

Just because you're finished the book doesn't mean this journey is over! You can continue to connect with me (@heatherboersma) and your sisters (@lettersfromabigsister) on Instagram where we post encouragement and equip you with tools to live your best life—the one God has planned for you.

We'd also love to hear from you. Send us an email or DM and let us know how this book impacted your life. What was one thing you read that changed the way you think about yourself or about God? What steps have you taken to apply what you've learned? Also, it would mean so much to our team if you left a review online, sharing what you loved about this book. The more we share, the more sisters we can reach with this message of hope!

I want to leave you with one truth before you slide this book onto your shelf or pass it on to your friend. You don't have to do anything to earn God's love. You are already more loved than you can possibly imagine. So please don't spend your life working *for* love, but rather work *from* the love you already possess.

Love your big sis,

Heather

There is love that came for us.
  Humbled to a sinners cross
You broke my shame + sinfulness
You rose again victorios